Industry in Action

General Editor   K. J. W. ALEXANDER
Professor of Economics and Head of
Department, University of Strathclyde

Advisory Board   J. E. T. ELDRIDGE
Professor of Sociology, University of
Glasgow

JOHN HUGHES
Vice Principal, Ruskin College, Oxford,
and Director of the Trade Union Research
Unit

RICHARD O'BRIEN
Director of Delta Metal Co; and Chairman
of the Employment Policy Committee of
the Confederation of British Industry

Man Mismanagement

Alan Fox

HUTCHINSON OF LONDON

HUTCHINSON & CO *(Publishers)* **LTD**
3 Fitzroy Square, London W1

London Melbourne Sydney Auckland
Wellington Johannesburg Cape Town
and agencies throughout the world

First published 1974
© Alan Fox, 1974

Set in Monotype Baskerville
Printed in Great Britain by
Ebenezer Baylis and Son Ltd., The Trinity Press,
Worcester, and London

ISBN 0 09 119590 X (cased)
      0 09 119591 8 (paper)

Contents

Contents

Editorial Foreword

A combination of factors make it difficult for the practising manager or trade unionist to form a broad and forward view of modern industrial society and his or her role within it. Pressures of work and living, narrowing specialisations, the increasing role of external influences particularly from government, and the pace and diversity of change all conspire against such understanding. The expanding demands of specialised functions have affected education and intellectual activity generally, compartmentalising thought and knowledge and in particular tending to exclude social issues and values and to isolate industrial theory and practice from society in a dangerously unreal way.

Despite welcome developments in both the quantity and quality of education for industry perspectives are still blocked by the preconceptions of yesterday and the preoccupations of today. Even the younger manager attending a course has to make a considerable effort first to widen his view and then to integrate all that comes within it. The books in this series *Industry in Action* are designed to complement the individual efforts of those managers, trade unionists, students and others who wish to take this wider view. Within the framework set by the need to understand the complex forces which are re-shaping industry and society each book will impart the specialist knowledge and techniques relevant to its area of interest and seek to establish and explore the links between the specialism and the technological, social, political and other influences which are relevant to them.

Industrial relations tend to be conducted on a day to day basis. Managements and trade unionists become totally absorbed in the details of the current crisis and in reaching some sort of agreement – often of a very temporary nature. The public, at some distance from the fray, see industrial relations as a succession of crises, with perhaps the details differing but essentially similar in character and form. It is almost as though the more directly a person is concerned with industrial relations the more difficult it is for him to see wood for the trees. Practitioners are too busy dealing with the current crisis or preparing for the next to take account of one obvious lesson of the series of recurrent crises we have become accustomed to: the need to look beyond the details of particular disputes to the more fundamental causes of industrial conflict.

This book performs that function. With admirable clarity and precision of thought Alan Fox probes deeply into the characteristics of our industrial society and the attitudes which pervade and poison it. This is not a book which offers easy solutions. Indeed it subjects some of the solutions on which great hopes have been placed to rigorous and often devastating critical analysis. Some readers may find the book undermines their confidence that simple and straightforward solutions exist to our industrial relations problems.

The virtue of the approach adopted in the book is that by arguing convincingly that the problems are so deep-seated it can encourage readers to begin a major re-appraisal, which must include a reconsideration of their own attitudes, of such issues as authority, power and equality. To force our attention beyond the incidents of industrial relations to its essence is the purpose and the achievement, of this book.

K.J.W.A.

Preface

Any man of our times can be forgiven, perhaps, for feeling that the problems and torments which men are apt to impose upon themselves and each other are multiplying more ominously now than in any previous epoch. Professional historians will soon spring to his elbow, however, to assure him that things were ever thus. Yet along one dimension, at least, they might be disposed to concede an unprecedented development, and a reader who is aware of it will be better equipped to appraise the themes and arguments deployed in the following pages. This change, profound and indeed explosive though it is, is soon stated. Over substantial and ever-widening portions of the globe, including the fragment we occupy, increasing numbers of people are demanding that their allotted span of life should yield them more than a mere slavish and anonymous preoccupation with survival. More and more they become conscious of a self and an identity that seeks nourishment not only through a share in the world's growing economic wealth but also through rising standards of health, education, status, respect, or whatever else they may see as giving meaning to their life.

We are only now beginning to discern the shattering long-term implications of this change upon social structures, institutions, and relations, both national and international. Over most of that vast span of history and pre-history during which man has painfully evolved his way of life, the lot of the vast majority has been such as to leave little time, energy, or resources for anything that we would now recognise as individual self-fulfilment. Scarcity, disease, natural disasters, the ever-present fear of death – these compelled men (as they do still in many places) to limit their hopes and their aspirations for themselves. But the application of science, technology, and purposive organisation to the mastery of nature has emancipated one section of humanity after another from its cramping compulsions, and with each advance the excitement and promise have spread ever more quickly to others who began to glimpse the vision for themselves and set themselves to pursue it. Viewed within the context of man's whole life on this planet, we are witnessing the gathering speed of an ever-widening human impulse towards an enhancement of individual life and experience.

Within this massive, long-term historical phenomenon – constituting the general background against which this book needs to be read – we can distinguish a separate but related trend which, while it affects as yet some societies far more than others, may well eventually overtake them all. This is the challenge to officially-constituted or conventional authority which increasingly displays itself in politics, in religious hierarchies, in universities and schools, in the family, and in the subject of this book: organisations of work. Here we come to the central theme of the discussions which follow. Men who seek to organise and control others have always had to choose what seemed to them appropriate strategies for securing compliance – and if circumstances rendered it desirable and possible, wholehearted cooperation – from those they organised and controlled. What is relatively new in human history is the growing disposition and ability among groups of men and women to examine the commands of those who seek to control them and, where they can mobilise the necessary collective strength, react to those commands in the light of their own needs and aspirations – not through convulsive and spontaneous gestures of revolt but through organised and calculated pressure on the policy-makers. The degree of challenge so far presented by this change to the existing social order in countries like our own is often exaggerated, both by those in whom it engenders hope for a more just society and by those in whom it arouses fear for their own power and privilege. But the long-term probability is of continuing change of great profundity, and whether one seeks to strengthen the controllers or resist them, the need for analysis cannot be ignored. As always, the first prerequisite for changing a situation in a desired direction is to understand it.

ALAN FOX

1. The Managerial Problem and its Context – Society and the Organisation

A visitor to a factory or any other place of work is soon aware of what might be called the 'material' technology. He sees people operating machines, applying tools, manipulating data-processing devices, using typewriters. This is the technology that can be seen, touched and heard, and is susceptible to the confident control and prediction of scientists, technologists and engineers. But it would all remain inert and unused without the application of another and totally different kind of technology: the 'social' technology which seeks to order the behaviour and relationships of these people in systematic purposive ways through an elaborate structure of coordination, control, motivation, and reward systems. This social technology, or social organisation, takes such forms as job definitions, pay structures, authority relations, communication and control systems, disciplinary codes and all the many other rules and decision-making procedures which seek to govern what work is done, how it is done, and the relationships which prevail between those doing it. How well this social organisation serves the purposes of those who seek to impose it depends in the last resort upon conceptions in the minds of the men and women they recruit for these purposes. It depends upon their conceptions of how they ought, or would be best advised in their own interests, to behave with respect to these top-management definitions of their duties and obligations, their rights and privileges, and their relationships to the material technology, to higher authority, and to each other.

At one extreme, the conceptions which rank and file bring to this management structure of rules and policies may lead them to work indifferently, regulate their own work behaviour in ways which obstruct management purposes, quietly subvert authority or openly challenge it, and totally withhold all spirit of loyalty to, or identification with, the company. At the other extreme, their responses may be such as to prompt them to work keenly and conscientiously, offer willing cooperation with management's leadership, submit readily to its command, and identify themselves loyally with the company. This combination of responses will be referred to throughout this book as 'moral involvement'. Between these two extremes lie many inter-mediate positions where rank-and-file employees offer a measure of passive compliance with orders but little more, demonstrating thereby neither a positive alienation from, nor a positive commitment to, the social technology which top management seeks to maintain for the pursuit of its purposes.

Employers and managements have always differed widely in terms of how high they pitched their hopes and requirements with respect to these conceptions which so shape the rank-and-file response to managerial rules and policies. They have, of course, been at one in demanding at least what they regarded as a minimum level of employee compliance with rules, orders and directives. But beyond this their behaviour has revealed diversity in the degree of their active concern to promote the more positive employee commitment and involvement just described. Some have devoted much effort to this end; others have allowed the issue to go by default.

We shall not concern ourselves in this book with the question of how far management in any given situation is well advised, in pursuing its objectives, to devote considerable resources to attempts at generating moral involvement among its employees. This is a complex issue too often oversimplified by advice manuals which take for granted that this kind of involvement is a universal necessity for managements in all types of industrial situation. In fact there are many variable factors to be taken into account in assessing how much of an effort in this direction is justified by *economic* values – factors which include technology and the type of productive system being used, the nature of the labour force, employee aspirations and attitudes, the state of the labour market, and various others. An attempt to elucidate these complexities would be a major distraction from our present task. This is to examine a range of strategies which management has applied to the problem of securing from rank-and-file employees whatever degree of compliance it deemed appropriate and, should its aspirations run that high, evoking also some desired level of moral involvement, identification and commitment. The strategies examined are all in use today, though their origins extend well back into our industrial history. They include coercive power, social conditioning, manipulative persuasion, unilateral attempts to gauge and satisfy employee 'needs' insofar as this serves management interests by evoking desirable employee attitudes, and, finally, bilateral consultation and negotiation between management and employee representatives designed to achieve mutually acceptable compromises, arrangements and understandings on a limited range of issues. We shall be asking, not whether the adoption (or non-adoption) of these given strategies was sound managerial judgement or not (for this depends on specific context), but what the assumptions and aims of each strategy are, whether in general it has succeeded or failed – and why.

Here we find ourselves in a vastly more complex and subtle world than that of material technology, for it is the world of that most complex and subtle of all organisms, *homo sapiens*. As soon as we deal in the motivations and responses of human beings and the relationships between them we lose the predictive confidence enjoyed by the natural scientist. The conceptions which men form of how they ought, or would be best advised in their own interests, to behave; the expectations they form as to the behaviour of others; the forces which help to shape such conceptions and expectations – these are far less easily studied and controlled than the behaviour of inanimate matter in the research laboratory. A sense of this complexity causes many a manager to shy away from any serious attempt to understand such a tricky and uncertain field and to fall back on traditional beliefs, popular assumptions and easy clichés, especially with respect to what will be our predominant concern here; his relations with the rank-and-file labour force.

Those who do try to deepen their understanding may be tempted to reduce the problem by confining their attention to what goes on within the organisation itself. They are encouraged in this by some training texts and advice manuals which limit their discussion of management/worker relations to this context.

Attention becomes focused on the organisation alone, to the exclusion of the wider society in which it is embedded. This exclusion is fatal for a full understanding of the issues involved. As we shall see, our journey of exploration into past, present and possible future management strategies, and into the reasons for the changing emphases we shall observe, takes us to the heart of fundamental questions about how men live together in society, what work experience means for men at different levels of the social hierarchy, and what changes, if any, are coming to bear upon the way men view these questions.

Organisational issues, conflicts and values are inextricably bound up with those of society at large. This has major implications for our inquiry. Prominent among them is that men's attitudes and behaviour towards their managerially-defined work roles, rights and obligations, and towards the roles, rights, and obligations of others, are not formed only within the organisation. They are formed also by the experiences, values, observations and aspirations which men acquire and construct for themselves in the wider society outside, and by the view they have thereby come to take of that society. Influential here are such factors as family, class, school, friends, locality, and the mass media of newspapers, radio and television. Thus the perspective they bring to bear upon the organisation and their place in it, and therefore the way they respond to its rules, rewards and values, is shaped by what they make of this wider frame of reference as well as by the organisation itself. There is, of course, nothing necessarily static about the perspective they hold. They may modify it as a consequence of their experience and observations either within the organisation or outside it. In any case it is obviously inadequate to try to understand workplace behaviour without also trying to understand the wider social setting and how men interpret it for themselves.

Two examples will suffice to illustrate the wide range of patterns of experience and perceptions. Even as he takes up his first job, a sixteen-year-old in a manual wage-earning family, for example, may have acquired from his school the assumption that he is destined to remain among the hewers of wood and drawers of water; from the experience of his father and other male relatives the conviction that work must be expected to be dull, frustrating and unrewarding except for the pay packet;

from his 'subculture' the view that 'they' in authority must always be regarded with cynicism and distrust in their policies towards 'us'; and from all the communications and influences brought to bear upon him by the media an unsettling vision of a vast array of life-enhancing goods and services which he is exhorted to acquire but which have, of course, to be paid for. Others approach their work life with a very different set of expectations. The son of a professional man or manager, going on at eighteen to university, may feel confident of becoming a manager or professional man himself, graduating up through an interesting, well-paid and high-status career in what he will see as an essentially benign society. He may well expect to be among those who control and make decisions for others, and to be able to share with relative ease in the modern cornucopia of material abundance. It need hardly be stressed that there are many variant sets of attitudes besides these which men can bring with them into the organisation, but it is not difficult to see that these alone produce widely differing perceptions and behaviour.

The implications of all this can now be made explicit. In examining managerial strategies for promoting employee compliance and involvement, we shall be less liable to overlook important aspects of both managerial and employee behaviour if we never lose sight of the wider social setting within which they conduct their mutual relations. Some attention to the latter is therefore desirable before we begin exploring the former. But the picture which confronts us is not a simple one.

TWO PERSPECTIVES ON THE NATURE OF WESTERN SOCIETY

The complexity evident in the make-up of *homo sapiens* is no less apparent in the societies he creates. It is one reason why political theorists and sociologists disagree on the real nature of Western industrial societies and how they actually work. Even scholars who share the same personal feelings about these societies may select different facts for emphasis or interpret the same facts differently. And there is a further complication. Those who in general approve and those who in general disapprove of these societies are even more likely to stress different features or interpret a given feature differently. We thus find ourselves with sharply divergent perspectives often infused with correspondingly divergent personal attitudes towards what is being studied.

These differences of observation and evaluation do not, of course, extend across the board. Certain propositions would command agreement, such as that the economic systems of Western societies are mostly privately-owned; that the minority public sector, too, is usually required to operate on commercial principles; that these economic systems are based on an extreme division of labour and are served by a 'free' labour market; and that welfare provisions help to relieve some of the casualties of the system. But beyond these and other agreed propositions sharp divergences soon emerge. The exposition can be simplified by presenting two notional composite pictures. One, which we shall label pluralist, offers an essentially benign view of how Western society operates. Applied to Britain, it would point out how, in the political sphere, the major interests of society receive organised institutional expression through the Conservative and Labour Parties. These, representing mainly (though not exclusively) property, wealth and management on the one hand, and the power of organised labour and the less well-off on the other, enjoy roughly equal but marginally fluctuating favour which gives them alternating access to the levers of power for governing the country. In the economic system as in the political, the liberal freedoms of speech and of combination ensure that democracy and a reasonable approximation to fairness prevail. Trade unionism enables labour to face the employers on something like equal terms – indeed, as many would argue, on superior terms: are not the unions dangerously near to running the country?

Collective bargaining is seen, from this view, as giving organised employees a fully fair (sometimes more than fair) opportunity to negotiate with management on terms and conditions of employment. It is also, of course, one of the strategies through which many managements have hoped to strengthen employee compliance, but this aspect will be explored later. At the moment we are concerned only to register its significance for the pluralist as one of the major institutions lending fairness and justification to our economic and social system. For it is often seen (though not by all pluralists) not only as levelling up

6

employee power to an acceptable approximation with that of management, but also as reinforcing government social welfare and redistributive policies in gradually reducing class differences. As a consequence of these changes, manual worker affluence is regarded as rendering the old class conceptions out of date. Social mobility and a supposed equality of opportunity are thought to add their weight to this great improvement in living standards to make an altogether more equal society. More and more it becomes possible for talent and hard work to reap their reward through an upward progress in what is sometimes called a meritocracy – a new aristocracy based on individual ability and effort instead of on birth and social rank. Business, meanwhile, is seen as having civilised itself: in place of the old ruthless search for profit maximisation is the recognition of diverse social responsibilities to employees, consumers and the public interest. Subject to the wilder spirits in the trade unions learning the good sense, moderation and responsibility already acquired by their more sober fellows and cooperating with management and government to promote economic growth and control inflation, society can continue its gradual evolution towards ever-rising prosperity for all.

Perhaps relatively few hold these views in the form of a consciously-articulated and coherent structure of beliefs and values. Such a picture or some variant of it is, however, implicit in the attitudes and behaviour of many. We often have to draw inferences from men's behaviour as to what they believe. True motivations are apt to lie deep, and men may act and express themselves for reasons which they would find difficult to bring to the conscious surface. Because of this we often have to describe them as behaving 'as if' they held certain beliefs – in this case a set of beliefs about society and how it operates.

The set briefly sketched above is likely, for obvious reasons, to have special appeal for the more favoured and comfortably placed, since it offers a view of society as a reasonable and fair system of arrangements within which individuals and groups engage in healthy, regulated competition for the good things of life. Such a view reassures the successful that they deserve their luxuries and, if accepted by the unsuccessful, leads them too to legitimise the system and continue to accept it as right and proper.

On the other hand, this whole perspective on the way our kind of society operates has been subjected by some observers to severe and damaging criticism from which we can construct another and very different composite picture. This 'radical' alternative does not accept that the lower strata of society have been able to mobilise political and economic strength sufficient to achieve a fair approximation to that of the rich and powerful. Labour governments, it holds, are severely limited in their aspirations for social change by an awareness that most strategic decision-making power remains in the hands of those in industry, business, commerce and finance who are unsympathetic to their views and who could use a variety of covert methods to frustrate their designs. Similarly, argues the radical view, the power of trade unions to challenge management successfully on any really fundamental feature of our economic system is vastly exaggerated. The unions can cause managements and governments alike considerable difficulties on some issues, but these are relatively marginal to the total structure and conduct of business enterprise, which persists in much the shape that the owners and controllers of resources desire. Moreover, in propagating the gospel of 'social responsibility' business is only making a virtue of necessity. It is not the salient values of business which have changed but the social environment within which it operates. Trade unions, 'public opinion', government, all now constrain business to be a little more accountable to other social interests. For business itself, financial success remains the touchstone whether the object is bigger dividends for shareholders, larger surpluses to finance growth, or higher status and reputation for managers. Trade unionism has made little impact upon this distribution of financial rewards as between the major interests of society. Collective bargaining has not substantially shifted the proportion of the national product going to wages and lower salaries, nor have welfare and other so-called redistributive policies had the equalising effects imputed to them. Still less has there been any significant shift in the distribution of wealth and property. Such movement towards a less unequal society as was traceable in the Forties has ceased and possibly even reversed. Poverty, bad housing and higher disease rates for the bottom strata have been 'rediscovered'. Opportunities for educational advancement are still heavily unequal as be-

tween middle-class and working-class children, who are disadvantaged in many ways now familiar to educationalists.

Thus, in place of a picture which presents society as moving
steadily and inevitably towards a broadly egalitarian middle-
class pattern within which men enjoy roughly comparable
opportunities and advantages, there emerges a less optimistic
interpretation. It sees a largely privately-owned economic system operating within a competitive, acquisitive society still
marked by great inequalities of power, wealth, income, status
and opportunity. These built-in structural inequalities ensure
their own perpetuation, thereby creating the remarkably persistent patterns of poverty and deprivation which survive such
good intentions as reforming governments bring to bear, and
which private-enterprise capitalism tends constantly to generate
rather than extinguish. Within this structure the wage-earner
and lower salary-earner are still very much at a disadvantage.
Society and its values, institutions and conventions still take
forms which create severe and wounding divisions and afford
the favoured groups ample facilities for defending their privileges. Against these defences, reforming governments, operating
by the Queensberry self-restraints of parliamentary democracy,
soon learn their own limitations. Reforms are indeed achieved,
and important ones, but the essential character of the system
remains.

The extent to which disadvantaged groups see society in
terms which imply a perspective of this sort naturally determines
how far they view it with distrust. In practice many appear to
operate with a mixture of cynicism and acceptance, combined
with scepticism about the chances of fundamental change. In
this respect as in others the well-placed groups derive an advantage from their command over resources and their greater
prestige, education and articulateness. These make it likely that
their own, more benign, pluralist view will effectively predominate, even to some extent among those strata who fare relatively
ill within the system. There need be no surprise, declares the
radical view, that so many of us pay more heed to the values,
principles and ideas of wealthy, powerful, high-status groups,
than to those of less well-off, relatively weak, low-status groups.

Such is the radical alternative to the pluralist perspective.
But what is the relevance of this debate for our main theme? It

9

is this – that the divergence of perspective on society as a whole is often expressed too in a comparable divergence of perspective on the social organisation of the industrial enterprise. Just as the former debate alerts us to a less familiar perspective on the general shape and workings of the wider society, so the same approach turned upon the industrial organisation confronts us with a comparably different perspective, and, of particular concern to us here, a different view of management's search for employee compliance and moral involvement.

A PLURALIST PERSPECTIVE ON THE BUSINESS ENTERPRISE

The pluralistic interpretation of the industrial organisation probably represents the received orthodoxy in many Western societies, even if it comes in a variety of versions. By this is meant not that it commands universal assent but that it is the view favoured, either explicitly or implicitly, by probably most persons of power, authority, status and influence who can be said to manifest a view at all.

Just as the pluralist perspective takes an essentially benign view of Western industrial society, so it takes a similar view of the work organisation. It sees the organisation as a coalition of interest groups presided over by a top management which serves the long-term needs of 'the organisation as a whole' by paying due concern to all the interests affected – employees, shareholders, consumers, the community, the 'national interest'. This involves management in holding the 'right' balance between the sometimes divergent claims of these participant interests. The possibility exists, however, that management, under pressure, say, from market competition or from shareholders, might pay insufficient heed to the needs and claims of its employees if they were not able to bring those needs and claims forcefully to its attention. Through collective organisation in trade unions, therefore, employees mobilise themselves to meet management on equal terms to negotiate the terms of their collaboration. The pluralist does not claim anything approaching perfection for this system. In some situations, imbalances of strength as between employers and unions or between management and particular work-groups may be such that for one side or the other justice is distinctly rough. They are not seen as so numerous or severe, however, as generally to discredit the system either from the unions' point of view or from management's.

We come here upon an implication of considerable importance that will recur at several points in our analysis. This is that the system of employers and unions, or management and unionised work-group, jointly negotiating terms and conditions of employment depends to some extent for its stability and health upon neither side feeling that it is being overly subjected to coercive dictation by the other. We can explain this by recalling a well-established proposition about power and promises. If someone extracts a promise from us by holding a pistol to our head, neither a legal nor a moral judgement regards that promise as binding in honour, and it is certain that we ourselves do not so regard it. As soon as the immediate threat is removed we feel justified in ignoring the promise, since it was extracted from us 'under duress'. Of course, were the threat to be maintained continuously – which might prove difficult and costly – we would continue to observe the required behaviour, but this observance would follow not from our recognition of a moral obligation but from expediency – from prudent calculation in the interests of avoiding punishment. Commitments and agreements which we feel to have been extracted from us under compulsion as a result of extreme weakness on our part do not evoke our sense of obligation so far as observance is concerned. What kinds of commitments and agreements *do* evoke such a sense of obligation? Only those in which we feel ourselves to have enjoyed adequate freedom in undertaking the commitment or concluding the agreement. And the sense of obligation is the greater the more nearly we approach a position of complete equality with the other party. When we accept the terms and conditions of an undertaking, not from any sense of being pressured or coerced, but from a sense of voluntarily agreeing to obligations whose nature and consequences we fully understand, we are conscious of a moral obligation bearing upon us. To be sure, we may sometimes be tempted to evade it, but when others appeal to us that the obligation exists – and seek to keep us to the line of duty by threatening penalties if we default – we do not consider the moral appeal to be irrelevant or the threatened penalties to be an offence against natural justice.

What is the relevance of all this to relationships between management and rank and file, and to the pluralist perspective on those relationships? First of all it casts light on those situations where rank-and-file employees are not collectively organised. Here the employee stands only in an individual contract relationship with his employer. The employer's superior economic power in this contract gives him, in many cases, correspondingly disproportionate ability to determine its terms. This was the predominant pattern during the earlier phases of industrialisation and has by no means disappeared. Yet men of substance were apt to defend this system with the palpable fiction that it represented free contract between master and man bargaining as equals in the labour market, and as such called for full and honourable discharge by the employee of his obligations towards the master. Whether or not particular employees saw this situation as fair and as calling for scrupulous observance, the passage of time saw a growing number of outside observers who regarded this degree of power disparity as socially unjust, and of course the trade unions were propagating this message from the start. As they gained in strength the notion spread that, by mobilising themselves collectively and presenting a united force, employees were gradually eliminating the acute imbalance of power between themselves and their employers. Collective bargaining developed through which both sides committed themselves to certain terms and conditions of employment, including procedures which defined the method of handling claims and grievances without resort to strikes, lockouts, or other forms of disruptive action.

The significance of our 'ethics' argument now emerges. To the extent that the terms and conditions of the employment contract are seen as being settled, not by the coercive power of the employer, but by free and equitable negotiation between parties of roughly comparable strength, employees can fairly be required to offer honourable observance of the agreements that result. Organised collective relations in industry have therefore developed to the accompaniment of the widely propagated assertion that both sides have a moral obligation to observe the agreements negotiated by their representative agencies. As we have already noted, this is not to say that a sense of moral obligation is, or need be, the only motive for observing agreements. Men may be punctilious in observance for reasons of expediency – or, in the phrase used earlier, prudent calculation. They may, for example, consider that it will serve their interests best in the long run ('Honesty is the best policy'); or that to default would expose them to penalties and give the other side a good excuse for defaulting also. But because these expediency motives rest on men's calculations of their own self-interest they are a somewhat uncertain basis for observance in a complex and constantly changing world, for men's views of where their self-interests lie may fluctuate during the span of an agreement, and in any case there may be differences between the perceived self-interests of a group of union members on the shop floor and the calculation made and negotiated on their behalf by union officers. A sense of being under a *moral* obligation to honour agreements can therefore help to sustain consent despite these fluctuations and differences – and if the outside observer sees the negotiation arrangements as fairly balanced he will be the readier to see employees penalised if they default.

We can illustrate this pluralist perspective by relating it to what is felt by many to be one of the major issues of industrial relations today. For many years now employers in Britain have been bitter in their denunciations of the so-called 'unconstitutional' strike – the strike undertaken by a work-group, with or without tacit support from union officers, in transgression of the official disputes procedure negotiated by union and employers. The written evidence submitted by the Confederation of British Industry to the Royal Commission on Trade Unions and Employers' Associations (1965–8) asserted that 'For many years employers have felt that the greatest single contribution which could be made to the better working of the industrial relations system would be better observance of agreements.' The attitudes taken by the pluralist on the moral issue here are clearly shaped by his assumptions about the distribution of power in society and industry. The belief that the powers of employers' associations and trade unions, and of management and unionised work-groups, are as fairly matched as can reasonably be hoped for in a complicated world, leads to the assertion that employees should always act 'responsibly' (i.e. in accordance with their obligations) by observing the terms of the agreements negotiated on their behalf. Some of those making this assertion argue that where employees flout agreements 'society' would be justified in penalising them in some way until they respect them. From this view, transgressors are seen either as lacking all sense of responsibility and obligation, or as having some psychological quirk which renders them anti-authority on principle, or as holding subversive political views which require them to render present institutions unworkable.

The general picture of industrial relations that could be drawn from this pluralistic approach is one which, though hardly free of conflict, contains mechanisms enabling the contending parties, not too unevenly matched, to negotiate their mutual accommodations in a manner appropriate to a society which aspires to industrial as well as political democracy. Within this framework, employees would be assumed to see management as simply discharging its necessary functions and receiving its rewards like any other group in the organisation. In carrying out its job it tries to apply certain principles which appear to rank as inevitable facts of life – for example that those doing more responsible work must receive larger incomes than those doing less responsible work, that those wielding authority should earn more than those under their command, and that the managerial function is of self-evidently higher status than manual labour. In performing its coordinative, directive and innovatory functions for society, management has to control and contain the possibly divergent, possibly excessive aspirations of the various subordinate groups which make up the enterprise. These efforts inevitably involve it in friction and dispute. Yet these are not unhealthy conflicts which rock the fundamentals of the system (about which men are taken to be generally agreed), but understandable divergences of the sort only to be expected in a free society. Collective bargaining enables most of them to be resolved in a tolerable manner, though to be sure it creates problems, as in all industrial countries, still to be resolved.

It is some such picture as this that we derive from applying a pluralist perspective to the work organisation. As already suggested, probably many of the more favoured members of our society find it, or some variant of it, a convincing and satisfying interpretation. Again, this is to say not that they interpret their experience in any ordered and articulated way, for people rarely arrange their beliefs so comprehensively unless pressed to do so, but rather that such a view can be said to be implicit in their attitudes and behaviour. If we ask, however, how many rank-and-file employees think, feel and act by such beliefs and assumptions the answer must be that we do not know, for we have remarkably little hard evidence as to how they see their world. What is certain is that there exists a variety of 'social images' of which this, or some approximation to it, is one. Another is the radical perspective now to be presented. Between them they illustrate the sharply contrasting views men may hold of the social and industrial scene, and the way in which these views affect their interpretation of events and consequently their behaviour.

A RADICAL PERSPECTIVE ON THE BUSINESS ENTERPRISE

The starting point for examining the radical view relates to the distribution of power. Like the pluralist interpretation, it emphasises the gross disparity of power between the employer and the individual employee. Lacking property or command over resources, the employee is totally dependent on being offered employment by owners or controllers – and a dependence relationship is a power relationship. From this position of weakness he has little ability to assert his needs and aspirations against those of the employer, who can therefore treat him not as an end in himself but as a means to the employer's own ends: as a commodity-resource to be used for purposes about which he is not consulted and which he may not share. Unlike the pluralist, however, the radical does not see the collective organisation of employees into trade unions as restoring a balance of power (or anything as yet approaching it) between the propertied and the propertyless. He may well agree that it mitigates the imbalance and thereby enables employees to challenge some kinds of management decision on issues of special and immediate importance for them. But a great imbalance remains, symptomised by the fact that there are many other types of management decision which employees might aspire to influence were they conscious of having the power to do so, but from which they are presently completely excluded.

The radical would agree, however, that appearances may sometimes suggest to the casual eye that, on the contrary, the imbalance is in the employees' favour – and certainly this is a widespread and popular impression. Is not management sometimes forced to its knees by a powerful union or organised work-group? But, says the radical, examine the issues which are and are not at stake even in the most titanic-seeming clash. The former revolve around wages, who does what work and under what conditions, who should join what union, and other matters which, though of great significance for both sides, do not touch the basic fundamentals of the system. Trade unions strive to effect marginal improvements in the lot of their members and to defend them against arbitrary management action. They do not – and here we come to the crucial point of what issues are *not* at stake in management/worker relations – attack management on such basic principles of the social and industrial framework as private property, the hierarchical nature of the organisation, the extreme division of labour, and the massive inequalities of financial reward, status, control and autonomy in work. Neither do they try to secure a foothold in the majority of decisions made within the organisation on such issues as management objectives, markets, capital investment, and rate of expansion. Very rarely do they seriously challenge such principles as the treatment of labour as a commodity to be hired or discarded at management's convenience.

Why, asks the radical, do they not challenge management on all these issues which may clearly have major significance for the work experience, rewards and life destinies of their members? The answer he offers is twofold. First, employee collectives (unions and organised work-groups) realise that while they can deploy enough economic power (i.e. the collective control of their own labour) and enjoy enough support from government and other sections of society to enable them to offer an effective challenge to management on a limited range of issues where their participation in decision-making is seen as legitimate, they would need to mobilise far more power than is customary at present if they were to achieve significantly larger aspirations.

For, faced with demands which in effect struck at the foundations of management power, privilege, values and objectives, management would draw not only upon its own full reserves of strength but also upon the support of other managements, employers' associations and sympathetic sections of society (including government), which were concerned to defend the *status quo*. Such a basic clash would soon reveal where ultimate power lay, and the present capacity of the rank and file for a mass mobilisation against the *status quo* would have to increase enormously for it to lie with the unions.

This leads into the second aspect of the radical's answer. A mobilisation of power on this scale would require great resources of will, determination, confidence and aspiration. Why are these resources not presently available to the unions? Because their members, quite apart from being conscious of having something to lose from such a clash, are still too much under the influence of social conditioning to venture a bid of these dimensions. To some extent they accept as valid the principles on which the work organisation is constructed and the conventions by which management operates it. If they doubt them at all it is certainly not with the universal unquestioning conviction that would be required for a successful onslaught against the full power of property and resource-control. But, says the radical, this acceptance, total or partial, of the principles and conventions of work organisation cannot realistically be seen as a free and informed choosing situation in which employees rationally examine alternative possibilities and make an unforced choice. As we saw, the vast majority who are without resources must seek access to resources owned or controlled by the few, and such is their relative weakness and dependence that they are constrained, for the most part, to accept the essential nature of work organisation as they find it. Power counts, too, in many indirect as well as direct ways. It was noted earlier that the values of wealth, position and status shape much of the content of public communication in newspapers, magazines, radio, television, advertising, public relations, education and training, all of which manifest either explicitly or implicitly these dominant ideas and assumptions and, equally important, define the terms and limits of current controversy and debate. Recognition of this does not require us to accept a conspiracy theory of history, simply to acknowledge that in a thousand different ways powerless men survive and possibly prosper by serving the interests, values and objectives of powerful men, and can usually find some method of salvaging their self-respect while doing so.

All this suggests that the approach of many rank-and-file employees probably consists of a low-key acceptance of the organisation's essential characteristics. They are encouraged to see them not only as necessary and inevitable but also as legitimate and right, and while they may be keenly conscious of grievances these are not so overwhelming as to drive them to condemn the system *in toto*. Yet their subordinate and inferior position generally precludes them from participating in it with enthusiasm and commitment, for they cannot help but see it as having been imposed on them. Cynicism and distrust of 'them' may not be far below the surface, coexisting with a disposition to make the best of things, to reflect that they could be worse, and to conclude that since hierarchy, subordination and inequality are so universal and enduring they are probably in some mysterious way inevitable. If these ideas are changing it is only very slowly. Meanwhile they probably play an important part in maintaining the relative passivity which so many among the lower ranks extend to the major features of the system in which they find themselves.

When employees 'accept', therefore, as they almost invariably do, the basic structure, principles and conventions of the work organisation, they do so not from free considered choice, but partly because they are aware of the superior power which supports that pattern of organisation and makes it seem inevitable, and partly because their social environment induces them in any case to see it as 'natural', 'realistic', and 'only to be expected'. They limit their union and work-group aspirations to influencing such managerial decisions as are immediately important to them and which experience has taught them are within reach through the medium of collective bargaining.

How do they themselves see this negotiating method? We have already noted one view of it as a process of joint regulation by parties of roughly comparable strength who agree the terms of their collaboration and who acknowledge the imperative of moral obligation as well as of self-interested expediency in the observance of the resulting agreements. Employees with a radical perspective cannot hold this view. For them, collective bargaining is at worst a mere façade behind which the employer continues to dictate terms, at best a means by which organised employees can get marginally to grips with their masters on some issues although still leaving the latter with the real reserves of power. These reserves they rarely need to use because society and its institutions and values continue to retain the configuration necessary for their interests. For employees with this view of the social and industrial scene, the severe inequalities of power which subject rank-and-file employees to an inferior and subordinate position exempt them from moral obligation to observe organisational rules which run specially counter to their own needs and interests. This applies no less to those rules which have been jointly negotiated, for even in this process the employees are seen as being at a great disadvantage.

As we have noted, the radical agrees that appearances may suggest the contrary. Do not wage and other settlements sometimes lie nearer the employees' preferred position than to that of the employer? The radical's reply would be that, quite apart from the fact that bargaining tactics and gamesmanship complicate, even for the participants, the issue of what their preferred positions are, the aspirations of employees are themselves shaped by their awareness of the employer's power and the need to be 'realistic'. Employees try to achieve what they feel to have some chance of achieving given the prevailing power relations. Their claims take into account their awareness of the employer's superior position. Thus, says the radical, appearances are misleading and in no way contradict the proposition that employees, even when unionised, remain in a greatly inferior power situation. Similar arguments can be turned upon those negotiated procedures for settling individual or group claims and grievances – procedures which, by ruling out strikes, overtime bans or other forms of direct action, seek to guarantee to management that no disruption of work occurs. Through such procedures, management commits itself, in effect, to hearing appeals against its decisions. But to secure this concession, employee groups (and their unions) must forgo such tactical ability as their position may afford them to put pressure upon management during the process. In this matter too, then, says the radical, management's superior power is able to shape arrangements to its liking.

Thus, while employees may be able to secure from the employer certain marginal improvements in their relatively lowly position and its rewards, that position is essentially imposed upon them by these great structural inequalities of property ownership and economic power, officially sanctioned and supported by the coercive forces of the state, and by Labour as well as by Conservative governments. What moral obligation, asks the radically-minded employee, does he owe the employer to obey organisational rules, when even those that are 'jointly agreed' have been negotiated within what is in fact a highly unequal power relationship? Rather does he feel justified in pressing every minor advantage, manipulating every rule, exploiting every loophole, harrying every managerial weakness or leniency in his continuous struggle against those whom he sees as exploiting his economic weakness for purposes about which he is not consulted.

MOTIVES FOR COMPLIANCE:
EXPEDIENCY AND OBLIGATION

Whether the radically-minded employee (or work-group) does or does not flout agreements and refuse to extend to the employer a spirit of give and take (the spirit which, in fact, to varying degrees characterises most work situations) depends on his calculations of expediency. Our preceding argument suggests why he may feel no sense of obligation in his relations with the employer or management. But expediency may induce him to behave in much the same way as someone who does. Relevant factors here can include a calculation that this will serve his long-term interests best, an awareness that to maintain a permanent guerrilla campaign against management may goad it into a massive retaliation exercise which it feels it has to win, and knowledge that sharp practice on his part deprives him of effective argument against similar behaviour by management. Yet, as we know from experience and observation, work-groups do not necessarily calculate that their net interests point in this direction. They may, for a variety of reasons, resort to very different behaviour.

The significance of a purely calculative or expediency approach to the procedures, disciplines and restraints associated with a stable collective bargaining situation is that, whereas an established and accepted moral obligation remains unvarying in what it admonishes us to do, the dictates of calculative expediency vary according to circumstances, mood, and who is making the assessment. An example can be offered which illustrates these differences. Let us suppose that a certain work-group and the appropriate full-time district officer accept that the disputes procedure of the company concerned, having been, as they see it, fairly negotiated, deserves the fullest possible moral observance. While this conviction holds, the group's adherence to procedure can be expected to take a certain amount of strain. Some decisions emanating from the procedure may be unpopular and men grumble, but the predominant opinion supports faithful observance of the agreement. But if their reading of the situation is that the disputes procedure in question, or the circumstances of its origins, are such that they cannot offer it their moral adhesion, their behaviour with respect to its provisions will be governed by expediency. They may, for example, observe them when in a weak position where they feel unable to do otherwise, and flout them when in a strong position where they are conscious of enjoying a temporary advantage over management on the issue in question. We would also expect the group's acceptance of the decisions or awards issuing from the procedure to be uncertain for, lacking moral adhesion to the system, their attitude is less likely to be able to take the strain of unfavourable outcomes. Finally, we must note the possibility that the work-group and the full-time official may make different calculations of expediency. The latter may work to what he considers a higher-order expediency than that shaping the responses of the rank and file. He may look beyond their immediate personal interest to the union's long-term relationship with the company, perhaps with an employers' association, or to its institutional interests *vis-à-vis* rival unions. The possibilities of conflict are apparent, for the officer may find difficulty in convincing his members when they ask why his reading of the situation should prevail over theirs.

One of the characteristics of an expediency approach is that any relevant participant can claim his assessment to be as valid as anyone else's. Divergences are equally sharp if rank-and-file members insist on an expediency approach while the full-time officer endorses the approach of the Trades Union Congress in its written evidence to the 1965–8 Royal Commission, where it declared that 'The General Council acknowledged, as would every responsible trade union leader, that procedure agreements embody promises and therefore should not be broken by any union representative.'*

The threat presented to authority, control and leadership when rank and file react to rules, agreements and contracts only from an expediency calculation unsupported by any sense of obligation renders understandable not only that *management* should be found urging the moral sanctity of agreements and commitments 'freely and voluntarily' entered into, but also that trade union leaders too, in their concern for observance, should sometimes feel the need to reinforce expediency with the unequivocal ethical message that agreements embody promises which ought to be kept. In this they are like all rulers who seek to control their subjects' behaviour. We are, for example, threatened with detection and punishment if we rob banks. But if authority relied on this expediency argument alone the numbers of those who fancied their chances of evading detection would probably rise. We are taught, therefore, that it is also morally wrong to rob banks. With a combination of these two arguments authority hopes to keep us under control.

The reasons why trade union leaders have normally been concerned with their members' observance of negotiated agreements will be examined later. Meanwhile we can note that for anyone wishing to urge the moral sanctity of an agreement of

* Among those leaders who have chanced to make this acknowledgement explicit in recent times is Mr Jack Jones, general secretary of the Transport and General Workers' Union. After drawing attention to the difficulties of guaranteeing absolute observance by the rank and file, he asserted that all 'a trade union leadership can do is bind itself in honour to try to observe the agreements it concludes with employers and this I believe in absolutely. In general the assurance we give to management is that we bind ourselves in honour – we will do our very best to see that the agreement is observed' (quoted in *Working for Ford*, by Huw Beynon, Penguin Books, 1973, p. 302).

any kind it is crucial, in most Western cultures at least, to be able to assert convincingly that the agreement in question was negotiated between parties of roughly comparable strength. For, as we have noted, to the extent that it is seen, or felt, to have been imposed by a markedly stronger party upon a weaker, the moral obligation bearing upon the latter will be felt to be that much the less. The significance for industrial relations of a belief that the negotiating parties are not so unequal in strength as to exempt the weaker from obligation is therefore apparent. It plays a useful supportive role for those concerned to promote stability and order in work relations. Insofar as employees themselves accept the belief, their observance of agreements is reinforced by their sense of obligation. Insofar as that vague and ill-defined entity, 'public opinion', accepts it there may be political support for coercing employee defaulters into what is seen as their moral duty. With this kind of support within reach, those anxious to maintain stability are less dependent upon employees' calculations of personal expediency.

It is understandable, therefore, that interpretations of society based on the assumption of an approximate balance of power between the principal interest groups tend to be popular among those concerned to ensure that existing institutions work as smoothly as possible. Again, no conscious calculation need be postulated, only a tendency for men to be attracted by doctrines and interpretations which accord with, and support, the preferences, values and objectives they already hold. Conversely, those strongly critical of the prevailing social and economic order are likely to be found rejecting interpretations which appear to support a view of society as composed of balanced interest groups fairly negotiating the terms of their collaboration.

The author has already indicated that he finds the radical view, or some version of it, more convincing than the one with which it has been compared. But vastly more important for the manager is to gauge the views held by his own labour force, and to bring to the level of conscious inspection the views he holds himself. Only when he realises that his attitudes and behaviour implicitly contain assumptions about society and organisation is he in a position to examine them and decide whether he finds them convincing. It can, of course, safely be repeated that only a tiny minority of us formulate our views in any conscious, articulated manner. Nevertheless, in our attitudes, responses and behaviour, we all express a general orientation of whose fuller implications we may be unaware. In this sense, some employee groups may display a general orientation carrying the implications labelled here as pluralist. But equally likely – and in the absence of reliable evidence this can be no more than an impression – is that many employee groups, unionised or not, consider themselves in a greatly inferior power position *vis-à-vis* their remote and impersonal top management, and that their observance of rules and agreements owes more to expediency than to any sense of obligation (though this does not imply that the latter is wholly absent).

What happens when such a group becomes specially frustrated or resentful while at the same time conscious of a modicum of strength is exemplified in those industries where management complains of unruly and disruptive behaviour in defiance of agreed procedures for the peaceful handling of issues in dispute. The groups in question are clearly, on those occasions, no longer defining expediency for themselves in terms of observing the formal procedures agreed by management and unions (designed as they are to restrain or delay the groups from using such strength as they can muster). While they may choose leaders with a clearly defined social philosophy based on rejection of the *status quo*, they themselves may be conscious only of resentment and frustration in a work situation which affords them little or no satisfaction apart from the pay packet; which subjects them to subordination, discipline and control for purposes they have not chosen and do not share; and which dominates them through decisions made remotely and impersonally on the assumption that they are instruments to be used and not ends in themselves.

Men with feelings like these often behave according to the implications of the radical view whether they consciously hold it or, as is more likely, not. Whether they act on these feelings in such ways as to cause difficulties for management depends on their aspirations, their job situation and how far it affords them scope for bringing pressure to bear, and on the extent to which they have the will to mobilise and exercise that pressure. The higher their score on these counts – which of course interact with each other – the greater the strain on any expediency calculation they may have made (or that has been made for them) to the effect that agreements should be punctiliously observed.

When men's adherence to constitutional procedure breaks under this strain they often come under moral condemnation for failing to honour the commitments signed in their name. A crucial question which such critics might well put to themselves here is whether the men concerned are capable of honouring *any* moral commitment. The simplest inquiry will usually reveal that in their other roles most of them are dutiful husbands, devoted fathers, loyal friends, steadfast workmates. Why, then, does this capacity for moral commitment sometimes appear to fail them in respect of their agreements with the company? The one answer which management seems determined to avoid is that, while other claims and other situations *can* command their moral adhesion, the company cannot. Yet the company does command the moral adhesion of many in the upper ranks of the hierarchy. Where it most demonstrably fails is in its appeal to the rank and file. Unless there is evidence that the rank and file are incapable of extending moral adhesion to anything, we must surely look for explanations of their defaulting behaviour in the very nature of their work situation as they experience and perceive it. We shall find ourselves driven back again and again in subsequent discussion to this widespread failure of the industrial enterprise to evoke the full moral involvement of the rank and file. We shall have occasion to note again, too, the overwhelming tendency among members of the favoured classes to explain this away by blaming the moral infirmity of manual wage-earners or lower salary-earners, rather than considering the possibility that the enterprise is so structured as to be largely incapable, in Western culture, of attracting strong rank-and-file commitment.

Meanwhile we conclude this chapter by noting that issues of profound significance have already emerged which will serve as the setting for our subsequent discussion. Having begun by raising the central theme, so crucial to employers and managements, of employee compliance and moral involvement, we then noted that attitudes and behaviour at work could not be fully understood without looking beyond the factory gates to the wider society. For the factory takes its structure, principles, beliefs and values from among those bred within, and in varying degrees nourished by, that wider society. But we then noted that these principles and beliefs do not constitute a homogeneous unity and consensus shared by everyone. Men diverge in how they interpret and evaluate social structures and institutions; they differ in their values and assumptions. Accordingly two contrasting perspectives were then presented, the pluralist and the radical, which demonstrated in what different terms men could perceive their society. It then became apparent that the same two perspectives could be turned upon the enterprise itself, resulting in very different consequences for how men see the organisational power structure and the whole pattern of relations between management and employees. This led us to examine certain crucial aspects of these relationships which bear especially upon our chosen theme – employee compliance with managerial rules, orders and directives. These aspects concern the two basic motives for obeying orders and observing rules – moral obligation and individual or group expediency. This discussion brought out the fact that the pluralist perspective on society and the enterprise must be seen not as socially neutral but as having great ideological significance. It presents an essentially benign view of society and the enterprise as deserving full legitimation by its members and thereby calling for their full moral adhesion on the basis of obligation rather than expediency. The alternative radical ideology disputes this interpretation and the author has indicated that he finds this challenge convincing.

His reasons for doing so will emerge cumulatively during succeeding chapters. For, having sketched the central theme and taken note of conflicting opinions about the social and organisational context within which it needs to be located, we must explore more fully the nature of the managerial problem we are concerned with here. Subsequently we shall discuss the various strategies employed by management to overcome it, the reasons for their relative success or failure, the explanations of the shifting emphasis observable over the years, and such possibilities as it seems sensible to visualise for the future.

Further Reading

CARTER, M. *Into Work*. Harmondsworth: Penguin Books, 1966.

CASTLES, F. G., MURRAY, D. J., POTTER, D. C. (eds) *Decisions, Organizations, and Society*. Harmondsworth: Penguin Books in association with The Open University Press, 1971.

FOX, ALAN. *A Sociology of Work in Industry*. London: Collier-Macmillan, 1971.

FOX, ALAN. 'Industrial Relations: A Social Critique of Pluralist Ideology' in *Man and Organization: The Search for Explanation and Social Relevance* (ed. J. Child). London: George Allen and Unwin, 1973.

GILBERT, M. (ed.) *The Modern Business Enterprise*. Harmondsworth: Penguin Books, 1972.

KERR, CLARK. 'Plant Sociology: The Elite and the Aborigines' in *Labor and Management in Industrial Society*. New York: Anchor Books, 1964.

PARKIN, F. *Class Inequality and Political Order*. London: Paladin, 1972.

PERROW, C. *Organizational Analysis: A Sociological View*. London: Tavistock, 1970.

WESTERGAARD, J. H. 'Sociology: the Myth of Classlessness' in *Ideology in Social Science* (ed. R. Blackburn). London: Fontana/Collins, 1972.

2. Coercion and its Limits

In bringing a closer focus to bear upon the managerial problem of securing employee compliance or, more ambitiously, moral involvement, we need to be clear about why such a problem should emerge in the first place. Many of the explanations offered over the years by persons of position and status, and still popular today, rest explicitly or implicitly upon the belief that rank-and-file employees lack the capacity to feel moral obligation, loyalty and commitment, or that they wilfully withhold them out of stupidity, irrational prejudice or political spite. It is understandable that those who most benefit from, and most identify with, our social and economic system should be loath to acknowledge even to themselves the possibility that the employee behaviours they deplore are an outcome neither of moral infirmity nor of stupidity, but of reactions to the social and work situations to which the system allocates most members of the wage-earning and lower salary-earning classes. Such an acknowledgement would leave the critics only the two alternatives of either stoically enduring the behaviours they deplore or changing the essential nature of the very system which endows them with their superior advantages and status. Since both are disagreeable there is a strong disposition to believe that these behaviours need not be stoically endured and can be transformed or at least changed markedly for the better by managerial strategies which leave the essential framework, character and values of the system intact.

Already, however, our discussion has brought out the argument that it is this framework and character of the industrial enterprise, and in certain major respects the society that contains it, which must bear the main responsibility for the failure to command to any substantial degree the moral adhesion of rank-and-file members. It is at this argument that we must now look more closely before we go on to examine the managerial strategies and assess the reasons for their relative success or failure. A fruitful way to begin, perhaps, is to explore further the possibility referred to in the preceding chapter – that rank-and-file employees may come to see themselves as being used for the purposes of others.

PROBLEM-SOLVING AND WIN-LOSE SITUATIONS

The full implications of this for their attitudes and behaviour can be brought out by comparing such a situation with a very different one. Let us suppose that we join as equals with a number of others in the pursuit of a common purpose. We soon discover it necessary for some to act in a leadership and coordinative capacity. Given the common purpose, we accept them and feel able to trust them in those roles. This is not to say that disagreements will not arise with respect to means. But given the shared ends, these disagreements can be handled in what is often called a 'problem-solving' manner. This means that attention will be directed to clarifying the facts, searching for the best methods, and elucidating the probable consequences of alternatives. The parties do not seek to trap, bluff or score off each other, for they all have an interest in pursuing the same objective. For the same reason, they do not conceal, distort or manipulate information and ideas. Communications are open and unscreened, for the parties trust each other. This problem-solving pattern can be described, in fact, as a high-trust pattern.

This may be compared with a situation in which men are conscious of submitting to superior power in being directed towards the pursuit of ends they do not fully share. Those in positions of dominance are clearly unlikely to command the full confidence of those they dominate, for their policies and decisions are directed to purposes which to some degree differ from those of the rank and file. In such a situation those who are controlled are conscious of being used as means to other people's ends. This is not a formula for high-trust relations. While those controlled may see the controllers as personally honourable men who practise straight dealing, this does not preclude a conviction that they must be carefully watched and ways found, if possible, of influencing certain aspects of their decision-making. In place of the open problem-solving and free communications between equals that are possible in the situation of shared goals, we are likely to see power manœuvres between unequals which display all the characteristics of low-trust relations – mutual suspicion, bargaining, gamesmanship, defensiveness and distorted communications. This is the pattern which in its more marked forms becomes a 'win-lose' situation where each party automatically defines a gain for the other as a loss to itself, and vice versa.

Asked to apply these two contrasting sets of notions to industry, the manager may urge that the former should be seen as the more appropriate. His reaction would be understandable. Who, in running a large complex organisation, would not prefer that the rank and file fully share his purposes and thereby feel able to trust his leadership, accept his authority, and extend full compliance with the rules, decisions and policies bearing upon them? Such hopes are rarely realised. More often he confronts some degree or other of low-trust response, and may be tempted to attribute it to stupidity, ignorance or moral weakness. We are none of us wholly free of these failings, but he would do better to take as his starting point the probability that, although they may trust him as a person, they do not feel fully able to trust him in his role as manager. What are the factors likely to generate this rank-and-file consciousness of being used as means for the pursuit of other men's purposes – purposes with which they feel unable to identify?

WHAT PREVENTS RANK AND FILE IDENTIFYING WITH MANAGEMENT?

To answer this we have to ask ourselves what changes in their position would prompt us to expect with some confidence that henceforth they would feel more ready to identify with top management's purposes and values. We would surely expect such identification if – after the appropriate training and personal adjustment – their jobs were to be redefined to embody much greater discretion, responsibility and autonomy, their position in the organisation changed so as to ensure them individual treatment based on personal respect, and their whole pattern of rewards and status shifted much nearer to those of top management. In such circumstances they would be far more likely to feel included as trusted and fully-participating members of a collective effort, and far more able, therefore, to identify with that effort and those who lead it.

What we have described, of course, are the circumstances in which most middle and senior managers, higher-level administrators and professionals of all kinds pursue their occupations. They are usually observed to be more identified and morally involved with their work situation than most wage- and lower salary-earners. The profoundly different low-discretion work circumstances of the latter cause them to feel excluded from more significant and responsible participation, and therefore not really trusted. Their inferior rewards (and the resistance usually offered by top management towards enlarging them) confirm their sense of being low-status 'hands' who are not seen as full members of the higher corporate effort. The old terminology of 'hands' and 'staff' embodied this crucial distinction. Current attempts to conjure with a new terminology which designates all groups as staff are unlikely to evoke the sought-for spirit of involvement so long as the realities of job, subordination and rewards remain the same. Rank-and-file members will continue to feel used by top management in ways which, by excluding them from significant participation in its purposes, render it unlikely that they will identify with those purposes. Admittedly it is not impossible for men who are totally excluded from significant participation in high purposes to identify with those purposes and behave accordingly. But such cases are rare. The private soldier who, in battle, identifies with the purposes of a High Command he never sees and which treats him as expendable is hardly an appropriate model for factory workers making pots, pans, cars and television sets for an anonymous commercial market. Their situation makes it all too probable that they will see top management's purposes as being in some respects alien to their own. Whether the purposes for which they feel used relate to private profit, managerial empire-building or some remote abstraction like 'the public interest', they are conscious that their needs and aspirations are being actively cultivated by management only insofar as this contributes to, or is

31

at least compatible with, its own top priority purposes. What *are* their needs and aspirations? Their inferiority of treatment along all the dimensions of well-being, together with the circumscribed nature of their role and their exclusion from the centres of power, knowledge, responsibility and control, are likely to push them towards a preoccupation with such aspects of their personal stake in the organisation as pay, working conditions, job arrangements and security.

This is not to suggest, as we hardly need reminding, that in being exploited by management to serve ends with which their lowly position and treatment make it difficult for them to identify they will necessarily be oppressed and totally deprived. Grossly ill-treated labour is not necessarily profitable or productive labour, though the history of slavery demonstrates that vast fortunes can be built on it in appropriate circumstances. More commonly the labour factor of production has been found to yield a higher return if certain of its interests and needs are considered. Strategies deriving from this discovery, such as industrial welfare and that of 'treating the worker as a human being', have often, as we shall see later, been hailed as growing signs of a moral ethic among businessmen. The argument developed here suggests that they are more convincingly seen as policies of expediency designed to render labour a more efficient, cooperative and committed productive resource. They have been pursued up to, but not beyond, the point at which businessmen saw diminishing returns setting in. However lavish the care devoted to employee needs and interests, such a policy remains within the strategy of treating labour as a means to managerial ends if its purpose is to evoke a more profitable or productive performance and is tapered off as soon as this return is no longer evident.

In recognising the likelihood that rank-and-file members will consider themselves used as means to other people's ends, we are suggesting the main cause for that absence of loyal and dedicated commitment of which management so often complains. Its manifestations range from passive indifference and negligent performance, through collective challenges and organised opposition, to active obstructionism and anti-authority strategies. These diverse expressions are, of course, complex phenomena which require careful analysis in order to reveal the reasons why each takes the form it does. But underlying them all are such objective facts about the rank-and-file situation as we have just been examining – the exclusion from all significant involvement in the higher functions and important policy-making, and the allocation of inferior rewards, status and respect.

MANAGEMENT AND THE SEARCH FOR LEGITIMACY

Given all this, however, there remains the need to appreciate that although employees may perceive themselves as being used for management ends there is no inevitability that they will express this awareness in behaviour or even consider the situation in any way untoward. Until relatively recently in our history many employees believed that deference to their master's will and interests was divinely ordained or at the very least an inevitable feature of that social station into which they had been born. Ruling groups in society not unnaturally directed considerable ideological efforts towards encouraging such beliefs, which were actively propagated from the church pulpit, the counting house, the magistrate's bench and the school. Where men accepted them they felt no aspirations to assert their needs and interests against those of the employer. No doubt part of their reason for accepting them was a consciousness of the great power of the ruling groups which dominated their lives. Consciousness of weakness can play an important part in causing subjected groups to accept the ideas of the powerful as proper and legitimate.

There is hardly need to point out to the modern manager that times have changed. The old deference patterns within which employees submitted meekly and unquestioningly to their employer's will have been dead in a few trades, occupations and industries for centuries, and though persistent in others until very much later are far rarer now. Many factors have wrought the change. Rising living standards, better education, and growing aspirations among ordinary men for self-respect and dignity have all contributed to an increasing disinclination to accept without scrutiny the commands, policies and decisions of officially constituted authority. Increasingly men ask 'Why?' Their *disposition* to do so has been sharpened by an increasing *ability* to

33

do so. Rising material standards and education not only quicken men's aspirations for more (on behalf of families and children as well as themselves), they also enhance the capacity for collective organisation through which some degree of power can be mobilised. Consciousness of this power itself stimulates new aspirations.

The decline in automatic respect for officially constituted authority is apparent not only in work organisations but also in schools, universities and the church. It is evident in many parts of the world and is unlikely to be reversed (though cultural patterns are still very diverse, and there remain industrial societies, for example Japan or West Germany, where willing receptiveness to managerial authority, leadership, policies and decisions is significantly greater than in our own). Managers in the West will find this factor increasingly one to be reckoned with, and will be expected by their masters, whoever they are, to devote more thought and energy to understanding the complexities and subtleties of their own social technology. How far they will be able to cope with this challenge without accepting fundamental changes in the social structure not only of the work organisation itself but also of society at large is a question which will become increasingly insistent as we pursue the arguments of this book.

None of this is meant to imply an absence of concern about this issue among managers in the present and the past. Rulers of all kinds in all societies and at all times have been, and are, much exercised as to how to secure legitimation from their subjects and thereby promote willing compliance with their rules, policies and decisions. One quite fundamental method has already been noted. They can use their superior command over men and resources to propagate a set of values and beliefs which inculcate respect and deference towards themselves, their system of rule, and the values and assumptions underlying it. They seek, in other words, to promote among their subjects an ideology which legitimises their dominant position. Soviet rulers emphasise the historic mission of the Communist Party in expressing the class dynamics of social evolution; Nazi leaders asserted themselves to be manifesting the will and destiny of the German Aryan race; British governments claim legitimation for their actions on the basis of democratic institutions, majority rule, and the ballot box. Businessmen and managers similarly have sought ideological reinforcement of their position. At various times and places they have asserted that compliance was owed to the superior social status of masters, the absolute rights of property ownership, the inherent prerogatives of the managerial function, or to the businessman's special skills and initiative in the production of goods and services. They have frequently enjoyed support from government, organised religion and many other institutions which help to mould our attitudes, such as schools, the law and the press.

These remain major conditioning influences in familiarising us as we grow up with the idea of accepting the rule and direction of other men. By the time the young adolescent takes up his first job he has been taught by a variety of agencies, including his own family, that this involves taking orders from superiors. Of course he will soon learn from his fellow employees, if they are union members, that there is a range of issues on which management's policies must be critically appraised and if necessary challenged collectively. But if he attempted to flout management rule on matters outside this range he would be told by the shop steward that he must not act the fool, that the boss has to tell people what to do in order to get things done, and that the union does not exist for the purpose of supporting indiscriminate individual kicks against the inevitable facts of working life. These 'inevitable facts' include extreme division of labour, hierarchical authority, structures of domination, and great inequalities of financial reward, status and intrinsic job satisfaction. In these ways trade unions, as well as all the other institutions previously mentioned, help to mould the employee towards accepting the idea of subordination. Were it not for this help that the manager receives from outside he would face a vastly greater problem in training and disciplining men to comply with the rules and constraints of present-day work organisation.

Even with this help many of his difficulties remain. Men may have been conditioned into a general acquiescence in hierarchy and subordination, but this is fully compatible with the consciousness that their work destiny involves being used as instruments by others for purposes (and through means) about which they have not been consulted. We have also noted that frequently, despite this general acquiescence which also owes much

35

to a sense of the futility of challenging the system, there arise particular issues immediately relevant to their welfare which stimulate them into opposition. These range wider, of course, than the familiar one of wage rates. A management decision to close a high-cost plant 'in order to rationalise production on the more efficient units' may result in a thousand of them being put on the dole, their living standards cut perhaps by two thirds. A new machine system is introduced 'to keep costs down' and they fear redundancy or the extinction of once-marketable skills. A new pay system is devised 'to reassert management control over inflationary wage drift', and they fear a pegging of earnings – and their shop stewards a loss of influence. A productivity agreement is proposed 'for the benefit of all' and craft groups ponder the wisdom of surrendering protective work practices which, once lost, may never be recovered.

For much of the time, of course, the issues are less dramatic than this. Many employees conscious of a divergence between management's objectives and their own simply become unable to feel any strong commitment to managerial rules, policies and decisions, still less to identify with their job in that spirit of dedicated loyalty which management would find so welcome. They respond indifferently to some rules, flout others, and generally interpret management's system of organisation according to their own divergent interests except when subjected to close supervision. Acquiescence by employees in the broad general principles of work organisation is therefore quite consistent with their positive challenge of some rules and decisions and their negative indifference towards others. Thus develops management's awareness of its problem with respect to compliance. What are the means by which different managements have sought and currently seek to solve this problem?

CONTROL THROUGH COERCION

Anyone trying to engineer full compliance with a given policy can choose between two basic strategies, or rather between different blends of those strategies. These are coercion and consent. At one theoretical extreme he can try to rely on an overt exercise of naked power to force men to do his will even though they would like to resist. Alternatively he can abjure the use of coercion thus defined and seek by some means (which may still require the exercise of power, though in less obvious and direct ways) to engineer their 'voluntary' observance of the policy in question. In the rest of this chapter we shall examine the use and likely consequences of seeking control through undisguised coercion.

Power for this purpose comes in many forms, but all derive in the final analysis from relationships of dependence. If someone is able to do me physical violence or subject me to physical constraint and I believe him to be prepared to use this advantage, my dependence for physical well-being and freedom on his goodwill is obvious. It is no less so if he controls resources to which I need access (e.g. for a livelihood), or if I want his respect, friendship or approval. Whatever it is I value, the degree of his ability to control the supply is the measure of my dependence upon him, and the measure of his ability to use it to pressure or coerce me into forms of behaviour I would not otherwise have chosen.* Dependence rarely exists, of course, wholly on one side – in the first case I may be able to inflict at least a minimal violence upon him, in the second the resource-controller may need something from me as well as I from him, and in the third the desire for respect, friendship or approval may be mutual. The important question is always, therefore, where the *balance* of power lies. Whose dependence is the greater? This is determined by the strength and urgency of the need on both sides, and the availability of alternative sources of supply for each of the two parties.

Whatever the nature of the dependence it creates a power relationship. The fear of violence or physical constraint, of being deprived of access to desired resources, of having respect, friendship or approval temporarily or permanently withheld – these are only selected examples of dependence relationships in which the advantaged party enjoys a position of power that he can exploit, if he chooses, to compel me to behave in certain preferred ways. What do we mean here by 'exploiting' power? He

* The term 'coercion' is sometimes fallaciously confined to the context of physical force. In fact, of course, any form of dependence is susceptible of being exploited to a degree experienced by the victim as coercive in its severity.

does not actually have to deprive me of whatever it is I depend on him for – the threat is usually enough. Nor do we mean by 'threat' that he continually needs to express it in words or gestures a belief on my part, derived from experience or hearsay, that he is prepared to exercise his power if necessary is often adequate to ensure that I study his preferences with some care. It is where the superiority of power confronting me is greatest that I shall be most careful in considering my actions, and where the power-holder may least need to make it visible or manifest. In personal relations the effects of power can be traced even further. The power-holder may, without even being aware of it, reveal signs of displeasure which I prefer to avoid by taking appropriate steps to prevent the cause. The effects of power are thus all-pervasive, and its manifestations range from brute physical violence to the subtlest nuances of facial expression and tone of voice. All can be found achieving their effects in work organisations if we include those based on slavery.

The advantaged party in a power relationship may not, of course, exploit his power. I may become convinced that he would never, in the slightest degree, use my dependence upon him to determine my behaviour in any way. Such situations do exist. The rare plantation overseer may have made it plain that he would never use his whip, the rare employer that he would never exploit the threat of the sack, the rare colleague that he would never use my need for his respect to influence my behaviour. More commonly those with power use it; some crudely and blatantly, others with subtlety and restraint.

The exercise of power varies greatly in the degree to which it is publicly visible. We are keenly aware of the strikers who picket a factory and prevent it from operating, for we see them on every television newsreel. We shall be much less aware of those who, six months later, decide to close it and throw them all out of work, for they are unlikely to be displayed on our screens. When a group of workers manifest power by forcing through a wage increase after a strike publicised with banner headlines every day for a month, we note this as a further twist to the inflationary spiral. When manufacturers, business executives and professionals 'adjust' fees, charges, prices or their own salaries they are far more likely to remain remote and anonymous. Wage-earners who impose stress and suffering upon a non-unionist by refusing to work with him can rarely avoid attention from the media. A dozen men round a boardroom table taking decisions which result in another company being forced out of business are not considered news. Even if they were, they are far better equipped to preserve their privilege of privacy.

In other words, some uses of power in our society are far more obvious and attract far more notice than others very much greater. Employee groups can affect management decisions on their own wages, working conditions, and sometimes production methods. In this they are the frequent subject of public comment, usually adverse. Far smaller executive and directorial groups take decisions on production programmes, prices, international plant locations, foreign trade, capital movements, credit terms and the money supply which significantly shape the fortunes of economic regions and indeed entire countries. Their activities come under much less public comment and what comment there is usually takes a measured, matter-of-fact and uncensorious tone. They are mostly presented as legitimate behaviours only to be expected from companies pursuing their legitimate interests within the rules of the system. It is difficult, for example, to recall any condemnation by the media of those who have greatly aggravated Britain's successive balance of payments crises by making profits out of currency movements against sterling. It is much less difficult to recall denunciations of strikers as selfish sectional groups using power unpatriotically to assert their own interests.

The point in noting these differences is to indicate what a distorted picture they create of the distribution of power. Reminded so often of such power as organised labour can muster, yet so rarely – and in such different terms – of the far greater power wielded by company boards in manufacturing, commerce and finance, we can be forgiven perhaps for accepting too readily the view which some may be eager to offer us of organised labour usurping rightful authority and becoming the overmighty estate. We shall not be able to think straight about such matters, however, unless we bear in mind that the palpable and visible exercise of coercion which tends to attract our attention is only one of the more obvious manifestations of power. Those uses of power which attract least notice are often the greater.

D

The exercise of control through coercive power has of course always played an important part in the rule by the few over the many. Its application in work organisations can be identified in its more blatant forms by recalling characteristic utterances by employers and foremen down the ages which have passed into the folklore of industrial life. They include: 'If you don't like the wages I pay then go elsewhere – there are men queueing up at the gate for a job'; 'You're not paid to think; you're paid to do as you're told'; and 'If you can't work harder than that there are plenty who will – go and collect your cards.' For every man directly assailed by such open threats there have been a hundred who did not need this experience to tell them where power lay and what its basis was – employer control over productive resources and therefore over access to a livelihood. Even though the power relationship might not be overtly manifest, the awareness of it shaped the behaviour of both parties.

Time has wrought some change. In many situations a more effective union organisation at the workplace, or the protections introduced by dismissal procedures, or simply, perhaps, a tighter labour market, have modified power relations in ways which are obliging management to mend its manners and act more circumspectly in its handling of men. Yet the essential power relations remain and the same processes continue, veiled now however by the politer euphemisms deemed desirable for public relations. Men are 'declared redundant', become 'surplus to requirements', are subject to a 'labour shakeout', come to be seen as 'not quite what the job needs'.

CONDITIONS OF EFFECTIVE COERCION

Such has been the reaction in recent times against the harsher, cruder and more overtly authoritarian modes of rule that some management writings have appeared to suggest that these modes are invariably less effective in terms of practical results than the more urbane and manipulative ways of exercising power we shall be examining later. No universal proposition on these lines can be sustained. Given simple routine tasks requiring little exercise of discretion, judgement or initiative, and a large supply of weak defenceless labour, coercive power can achieve considerable results provided there is enough of it and that it is used sufficiently ruthlessly. The extreme case has already been mentioned. The vast fortunes of some of the English landed aristocracy were derived from plantation slavery in the West Indies and elsewhere, so their descendants could be permitted a smile at the proposition that naked coercion does not pay. Even short of that extreme, which included, of course, physical violence, coercion was able to secure perfectly adequate results for many an entrepreneur during the Industrial Revolution in Britain and elsewhere. What have just been suggested as the conditions in which coercion can be a perfectly viable instrument of policy if profits or output are the only criterion were in fact exactly those prevailing in some industries during earlier industrialisation – thus the origins of the term 'wage-slavery'.

Both the conditions referred to above are indispensable. Coercion is well known to evoke all those negative responses referred to collectively as 'alienation', along with resentment, frustration and a disposition to evade performance of duties except when under immediate supervision and threat of punishment. These do not necessarily, however, destroy or even seriously detract from the profitability of the system. Having 'enough' power means being able to maintain constant supervision and punish instantly any tendency among employees to allow their negative feelings to have adverse effects on their work performance. If we translate this into modern terms we must imagine a power disparity so extreme that the employer feels free to discharge at once any employee guilty of absenteeism, lateness, obstructiveness and anything less than maximum performance. Few can indulge today in such luxury, but there have been situations in our industrial history which bore some approximation to this pattern for varying periods of time. But even this does not indicate the full degree of power necessary for a policy of total coercion. If those being coerced, though weak as individuals, are able to mobilise enough *collective* strength to strike back in some manner at their exploiters, the latter must set against the benefits they derive from the system the costs which result from this retaliation. It then becomes conceivable that the costs may in time begin to outweigh the benefits. The employer's power superiority must therefore be sufficient not only to crush all individual resistance to his coercive rule if the policy is to succeed, but also to destroy all collective challenges as well.

This brings us to the second condition. If the tasks to be done call for a significant measure of discretion, judgement or initiative, the limits of usefulness of the coercion strategy are much more quickly reached. A man can be coerced into performing routine physical movements with regularity and speed. But he cannot be coerced into making good judgements, exercising initiative or using his discretion creatively in the service of another person's objectives. Good judgements and creative initiatives spring from cooperative high-trust responses which involve his mind and spirit as well as his physical self. Faced with the aggressive, low-trust hostility and attempted compulsion embodied in the coercive exercise of power, his self-protective and defensive responses predominate instead. The greater the discretionary content of the job, therefore, the greater the likelihood that coercive, authoritarian patterns of management and control will, by alienating the occupant, render him incapable of those states of mind and spirit desirable for the quality of decisions sought by management. Conversely the lower the discretionary content the less it matters for management, other things being equal, what the state of mind is of the job occupant. The more the job can be reduced to routine physical movements involving only minimal discretion, the more coercive control can be applied, for the less it matters to management if the employee's resources of mind and spirit are impoverished and alienated.

WHEN DOES COERCION FAIL?

But in a world of change other things do not remain equal. Rising aspirations among occupants of low-discretion jobs for dignity and self-respect dispose them to be more resistant to coercive methods and policies. As individuals they may, if the state of local labour markets permit, manifest their dissatisfaction overtly by being resistant and obstructive, or reveal their alienated indifference through high absence, sickness and wastage rates, or in the extreme case vote with their feet by getting work elsewhere. Where they find collective organisation possible they challenge the terms and conditions of employment which management seeks to impose on them, and may be supported in this by legislation, public policy and public opinion. These responses raise the costs for management of blatantly coercive authoritarian methods and styles and prompt a search for other means by which it can pursue its ends without incurring such costs.

There is another reason for a shift in managerial perspective. In some industries it has become increasingly difficult for management to rest content with a passive, alienated indifference among its rank-and-file labour force. Even on the assumption that its power superiority is sufficient to continue enforcing compliance with low-discretion, routine task behaviours, changing circumstances may call for more than passive uninvolvement even among those performing these humble jobs. Quickening foreign competition and accelerating technical change may require, from management's point of view, a ready and cooperative acceptance by rank and file of adaptation and flexibility. But such responses are unlikely to be forthcoming from those conscious of being coerced in their work roles by superior management power. Rank-and-file attitudes and habituated behaviours bred of earlier coercive work relations may prove costly for management when the need arises for accommodative responses which cannot be wrung from them by sheer power (even assuming it to be available). Management's requirements may change in yet other ways. Not only may there develop a need for ready acceptance of new methods, techniques or technologies, but the new technologies themselves may require a greater involvement and sense of responsibility on the part of the employee if they are to yield management their full potential return.

The reasons now become apparent why management may find an overtly coercive strategy inappropriate to its needs. In the first place, the changing nature of the required task behaviours (which can include the requirement of a cooperative receptivity towards change and adaptation) can render them quite incongruent with such a strategy. The more top management requires of a given job role that the occupant display judgement, initiative, commitment to top management goals and identification with the organisation, the less likely it is to use open coercion

43

in its dealings with him. The nearer we direct our attention to the top of the hierarchy, the more we find seniors being treated by top management not as persons to be subjected to authoritarian discipline and coercion but as members of a fraternity who are assumed to be sharing certain objectives and who must be handled with respect.

Underlying this strategy are, in the final analysis, power considerations. For top management to subject the occupant of a high-discretion role to authoritarian discipline and coercion is to run a risk, not simply that he will fail to exercise his discretion in the service of top management's interests, but that he will exercise it actively in opposition to them. Special importance is therefore attached to his identifying with top management goals and values. For this reason alone, if for no other, we would have to expect the occupant of a role in the upper strata, possessing as he does greater individual autonomy to use for or against top management interests, to receive far more generous treatment than those in the lower strata. In other words, by virtue of the very job role allocated him, he has power against top management in the sense that he could, if he chose, use his job discretion – perhaps for some time before the fact was discovered – in ways which could do it considerable harm.

By contrast, the occupant of a low-discretion job at the bottom of the hierarchy has far less opportunity as an individual to effect such damage. To be sure, his ability to raise the cost to management of openly-coercive strategies has in many situations increased. As we have noted, such responses as high turnover, absence, sickness and wastage may emerge as individual forms of protest (though they can have additional or different causes) which are not easily suppressed, in the present context of social values and attitudes, by methods of naked coercion. But top management only begins to feel the power of these responses when they are practised by significantly large numbers of employees – when they begin to approximate, in other words, to something like collective expressions of protest. The individual by himself can make little impact on management through such behaviours. Similarly his discharge of his actual job tasks affords him, as an individual, far less scope for injuring top management's interests than is available to occupants of high-discretion roles. His freedom of choice is much smaller, and in any case should he use it in ways damaging to top management objectives his actions will be more quickly detected. These facts simply describe a situation in which he has far less power than the occupant of a high-discretion job and is that much less likely to have his interests carefully and spontaneously considered by top management. It is for this reason that he feels he has to combine with his fellows to bring collective pressure upon management if his interests are to be fully considered. Aware that top management is using its power coercively to impose terms and conditions of employment and work rules and disciplines, they mobilise what power they can to oppose this process and oblige the decision-makers to modify their policies.

Historically, this kind of collective response has led many employers and managements to feel that in their own interests they must moderate their use of coercion and authoritarianism and search for other ways of promoting compliance among rank and file. Thus whether we are examining high-level, high-discretion jobs or low-level, low-discretion jobs, power considerations play a major part in inducing top management to seek other methods than overt coercion as a strategy. To a consideration of these other methods we turn in the next chapter.

Further Reading

BENDIX, R. *Work and Authority in Industry.* New York and Evanston: Harper Torchbooks, 1963.

FOX, ALAN. *Beyond Contract: Work, Power, and Trust Relations.* London: Faber and Faber, 1974.

KAHN, R. L., BOULDING, E. *Power and Conflict in Organizations.* London: Tavistock, 1964.

ROTHSCHILD, K. W. (ed.) *Power in Economics.* Harmondsworth: Penguin Books, 1971.

TANNENBAUM, A. S. *Social Psychology of the Work Organization.* London: Tavistock, 1966.

YOSHINO, M. Y. *Japan's Managerial System.* Cambridge (Mass): Massachusetts Institute of Technology, 1971.

3. Industrialisation and the Strategy of Consent

We have seen that a coercion strategy which may serve top management well given an abundant and defenceless labour force and tasks requiring mainly routine physical movements is likely to lose its appeal when these conditions are no longer met. If task definitions change in such ways as to require more of the individual than the repetition of physical movements, the alienating consequences of coercive and authoritarian strategies may well preclude him from being willing or able to offer the greater contribution required. Even if tasks remain the same, an increase in the power of those performing them – achieved through combination or labour scarcity or both – makes possible retaliatory behaviours of a wide variety of kinds, such as trade unionism, indifferent performance, obstructiveness, or higher turnover, absence, sickness or wastage rates.

But what is the alternative to this coercive strategy by which the employer seeks compliance through overt threats and exercise of his superior power? We earlier noted the alternative as being a strategy of seeking consent. In practice, management strategy is always a blend of consent and coercion, though the nature of the blend varies as between companies and between the various levels within each company hierarchy. The 'mix' usually reveals relatively more coercion at the bottom, relatively more consent towards the top. Consent covers a wide range of diverse forms and this chapter will be devoted to some of the more important. But first we need to note some considerations bearing on the notion of consent itself.

The essential meaning of power as the word was used earlier carries the connotation that sanctions are being used to pressure or coerce men into submitting to certain systems of rules and patterns of behaviour against their own preferences. But this is manifestly not the only basis on which men may work to systems of rules and patterns of behaviour. They may accept these without being coerced and without needing constant supervision, inspection and direct control by higher command. Here we examine the opposite theoretical extreme to that of total coercion. In this situation we might say that men fully legitimise management's rule. In other words, they offer full consent to it and to the policies and decisions through which it is expressed, so that management no longer needs to coerce. Spared the need to coerce, it avoids the negative consequences and retaliatory responses which so often result. We might say that the implication of employees giving full consent is that they 'authorise' management to govern them, thereby giving a special significance to the term 'authority'. Management can govern without this authorisation by employing coercion, but it faces at best passive indifference and at worst militant hostility. The value to management of consent is therefore apparent.

The most attractive picture of consent so far as management is concerned bears the characteristics of the model sketched in the opening pages of the preceding chapter. This envisages the members of an organisation pursuing common objectives and, in the interests of this shared purpose, willingly accepting leadership, direction and coordination by those appointed to serve these indispensable functions. Any disagreements are clarified by rational problem-solving methods to which the relevant parties contribute facts, ideas and alternative proposals, the ultimate resolution being made by reference to what will serve best the common objectives. In such a situation, management's authority, as we have defined it, prevails throughout. Coercion is unnecessary, for this is required only when employees would otherwise pursue goals, policies or behaviours different from those preferred by management, and this by definition is not a characteristic of the type of situation now being described.

We have noted that by the time the rank-and-file employee takes up his first job he is already, to some extent, socially conditioned in this direction. A wide diversity of influences have accustomed him to offer a generalised legitimation of many aspects of managerial rule and of the type of organisation within which he is to earn his living. But issues and problems arise which are specific to the actual organisation in which he works and about which he may well be disposed to challenge management policies. Moreover the very nature of the work he does, limited as it is in terms of discretion, judgement, autonomy and intrinsic interest, and far removed from the centres of power, involvement and privilege, can well fail to arouse the positive commitment hoped for by top management. Additional efforts are thus felt to be needed at the organisational level to supplement and reinforce the influences brought to bear in the wider social setting.

So now we must review the more important means by which employers and managements have sought to promote full compliance with, and legitimation of, their rule, including if possible that positive involvement and identification which is often their ideal. Most of these means are still to be found in use to some degree, so in taking a retrospective view we shall also be taking stock of a wide diversity of strategies currently being applied.

PRE-INDUSTRIAL WORK RELATIONS

To find our starting point we need to go back even to preindustrial times, for there are still small workshops where prevails a pattern of relationships bearing some resemblance to that of a very much earlier age. The pre-industrial workshop, with its master, journeymen and apprentices, served a society marked by much poverty, deprivation, disease and superstition – and indeed by much brutal exploitation – but this is not all that needs to be said. The division of labour was, by our standards, minimal, and the small scale of operations made possible a personalised set of relations between the master and, as they were often then called, his servants. To be sure, personalised relations are not necessarily good relations – the small master could sometimes be harsh and tyrannical. But at its best the system could display a not ignoble reciprocity by which the master exercised a diffuse concern over his employees, taking into account their moral and physical welfare as well as the development of their craft skills, and they returned a diffuse loyalty going beyond the narrow calculations of self-interest characteristic of a purely contractual relationship. These manifestations of reciprocal goodwill softened the edges of the essential core of master-servant relations – the doctrine of obedience. The very terms carry the message so vehemently asserted by all those in positions of authority – that subordinates owed unquestioning deference to the commands of their masters.

In suggesting that an approximation to this pre-industrial pattern survives here and there today we refer, of course, to the spirit of diffuse give and take which can still prevail in small establishments. These are often marked by characteristics which make it possible for the employer, should he choose to do so, to foster personalised relations of a sort very much to his advantage. The small scale of operations often results in jobs being less specialised: employees enjoy greater variety and discretion in their work, relationships can be less structured and more informal. They are also likely to be more diffuse, and this brings us to the spirit of give and take. What we usually mean by this phrase is that the two parties to the relationship do not try to hold each other rigidly to some predetermined set of specific contract terms. One may request a favour in the confident knowledge that the other will not demand immediate and equivalent reciprocation, but will grant the favour knowing that in the long run it will be returned when an appropriate occasion arises. Thus an employee may agree to work overtime without extra pay to complete a job, confident that if later he seeks an afternoon off without loss of pay to pursue some private purpose he will not be refused.

In such situations the parties trust each other to observe a diffuse (i.e. non-specific) pattern of mutual obligations. The nature of what each owes the other is not precisely defined and each trusts the other to maintain a reciprocity over the long term. Of course either side may betray this trust. The employee may repay considerate treatment with indifferent work; the employer may repay long devoted service with a lay-off during a slack time. Such failures of reciprocity are likely to destroy the bond. But otherwise the reciprocal honouring of trust maintains and, over time, strengthens it. Such are the features of what we might call a high-trust relationship.

AN IDEALISATION OF THE PAST?

We must not, however, paint too rosy a picture of the small-scale work organisation. If we see a group of men cooperating as equals in the pursuit of a common purpose, some accepting the functional need to subordinate themselves to leadership and coordination by others, and all being prepared to meet each other's temporary contingencies in a spirit of give and take, we are right to consider this a high-quality pattern of human association. It is a high-quality pattern because it is a high-trust pattern. But the small work establishment may fall far short of this noble ideal. Underlying it may be a grossly unequal power relationship. The handful of employees may be economically heavily dependent upon the employer. Yet the personal relationship he has with each makes it difficult for them to combine against him. The mutual reinforcement, anonymity and depersonalisation which facilitate unionisation in the large factory are denied them. Each stands in a face-to-face relationship with the man on whose favour their security depends. It is not easy for a person in such a position to pit himself against his employer in that stance of potential challenge which effective trade unionism implies. Instead he adapts to his position of weakness, feeling – though not necessarily from conscious calculation – that if he cannot secure his interests through an assertion of strength he must do so by identifying with his employer and hoping that this will evoke in return an adequate measure of consideration. The employer, if shrewd and well-disposed, encourages this pattern. By extending humane treatment and promoting reciprocal give and take he builds up among his employees sentiments of loyalty and commitment which serve him in good stead.

Such a pattern of human association is not to be despised. There are many worse patterns. Yet it is open to the criticism which can be made of all relationships which rest on a highly unequal dependence of one party upon another. They are potentially demeaning to the weaker participant. He cannot take part as a free and equal agent in the mutual determination of the relationship. His weakness leads him to subordinate legitimate needs of his own to the interests of the other, to anticipate over-anxiously the other's wishes and preferences, and to adapt his own values and aspirations in such a way as to evoke approval. All these behaviours are gratifying to the ego and interests of the power-holder, who is apt to see them as spontaneous tributes to his own excellence rather than as manifestations which would still be forthcoming even were he half-witted. They betray, however, the highest standards of achievement in human relationships, which have to be defined in terms of equality of power and thereby of dignity and respect. Failing this equality, the moral standard of the relationship must always be suspect.

However much master-servant relations or employer-employee relations display outward characteristics of mutual trust and respect, they remain subject to proof if they rest on highly unequal power relations, for they have never been put to the test. And the necessary test can be expressed in the question: would the weaker party be content with the same pattern of relations – with the same allocation of rights and obligations, privileges and duties, status and respect – were he suddenly to find himself vested with an equal degree of power? If there is reason to believe he would not, the relationship stands revealed as resting on nothing more noble than the ability of one man to dominate another. A central principle of Western liberal culture – that the priceless value of the individual personality demands social institutions which provide free and equal scope for its expression and development – is being manifestly dishonoured. The situation would be one in which the individual, freed from the constraints imposed by weakness and seeking now his full stature, finds his present roles and relations cramping and demeaning. Only equality enables him to make this judgement – or to decide, conversely, that his aspirations and purposes are such that he can legitimise on a free and equal basis what he might be thought to have accepted previously only from weakness.

We see, then, that judgements on the quality of human relationships are more complex than they may seem. The pre-industrial workshop has often been judged a good deal more wholesome in this respect than many modern work situations, and perhaps it was. Certainly it is often suggested to us that the mutual respect which, at its best, marked the relationship of master and man, squire and labourer, parson and villager, was superior to the competitive conflict of today. Yet evidence is abundant that when the weaker parties to these relationships found themselves in a stronger position or were able to mobilise themselves collectively they were prompt to demand changes in at least certain terms of the relationship. Perhaps the same would prove true today of many workers in small establishments where, on outward appearance, they seem fully to legitimise the rule of the employer and to be willingly receptive of their position and its rewards.

THE IMPACT OF INDUSTRIALISATION

If it were to be true that such diffuse, high-trust reciprocations as did redeem pre-industrial work patterns rested in any case on a basis of very unequal power relations, then we would have to say that industrialisation proceeded on a similar basis and moreover rendered these diffuse relations in many cases increasingly difficult to maintain even where employers would have liked to do so. Industrialisation took many expressions, but prominent among them were an increasing division and mobility of labour, growing size in scale of operations, the development of larger and increasingly impersonal markets (including that for labour), the quickening of competition, and the emergence of ideologies which legitimised and encouraged the pursuit of individual self-interest in the acquisition of money, status and power.

The combined effect of these and other associated features was greatly to weaken such diffuse relations as prevailed between master and man. The timing of this effect varied widely as between different industries and trades for the obvious reason that industrialisation proceeded at greatly differing speeds throughout the various sectors of the economy. Moreover the old traditional pattern of relations sometimes survived in vestigial form even in the face of growing size and new technology – there were always some manufacturers and businessmen who sought to preserve a paternalistic concern for their employees' welfare in the belief (sometimes justified) that this would ensure their loyalty and devoted service. But in substantial sectors of economic life there began to emerge what was to prove the characteristic pattern of employer-employee relations in Wes-

tern industrial society – a pattern marked by increasingly impersonal and narrowly contractual attitudes and behaviour, by
mutual distrust and grudging calculation, and by the decay of
whatever diffuse bonds of obligation might have mitigated the
harshness of power relations in earlier times.

The reasons why the hard lines of power domination were
now showing through more clearly and strongly can be traced
to the structural changes just enumerated. The increasing size
of work organisation represented a growing concentration of
economic resources which meant correspondingly greater power
for those in control, and the exercise of this power was less and
less muffled by whatever traditional obligations might have
restrained it in the past. It was directed towards constructing
and upholding organisations marked by increasing imperson-
ality of relations between master and man: division of labour
defined subordinate tasks ever more narrowly and specifically,
and was drawn towards close and often harsh supervision for the
enforcement of these low-discretion task rules. The diffuse work
roles and relations which had been acceptable to – and perhaps
even appropriate for – employers in the days of minimal division
of labour, local personalised markets and relatively static traditional communities were not acceptable for pursuing profit in a
world of expanding markets, large factories and increasing division of labour. Employers sought rather to make job definitions
more specific, work rules tighter, authority relations more clear-
cut, discipline more impersonal.

There was little room in all this for personalised bonds between
master and man. Even where an employer saw value or benefit
in trying to build up diffuse obligations of loyalty between
himself and his employees, he found it difficult – and the results
of his efforts increasingly artificial – in the circumstances of the
large factory. Many nineteenth-century employers were, of
course, only too glad to be assured that the general welfare of
employees was no concern of theirs. Such an assurance was
offered them by the social philosophy now favoured by many.
It saw the employer and the individual worker as free and equal
agents who bargained the contractual terms of their relationship
as 'economic' men unfettered by irrelevant non-economic ties,
bonds or obligations. Beyond observing the terms of the contract,
employers owed no further debts to employees. They could

abandon the notion – vague though it might be and honoured perhaps as much in the breach as in the observance – that they were responsible in something more than a narrowly contractual manner for the welfare of their workers.

CONTRACT AND MASTER-SERVANT RELATIONS

But if the spread of the spirit of contract was gradually releasing the employer from traditional obligations towards the employee, it brought no such gains for the employee. For his part, contract was being interpreted as requiring him to go on offering his master a general and diffuse obedience along with a spirit of loyal and devoted service. In other words, injected into the notion of contract were all the traditional 'status' conceptions of master-servant relations. The status of the master and the duty of obedience which was read into the employment contract were urged upon the employee in the hope that he would thereby legitimise the employer's rule and comply willingly with his commands and policies. This was tantamount to the hope that although the employer was imposing more narrowly defined job roles, closer supervision and more restrictive discipline, the employee would continue to return the same diffuse loyalties as had been possible under earlier work patterns.

We can express the same proposition in terms of trust relations. In describing traditional work patterns we characterised the situation at its best as one of high-trust relations. By this was meant that on the basis of simple technology, minimal division of labour, high-discretion jobs, personalised face-to-face contacts, local markets, and only the mildest of competitive pressures, master and man could, if they chose, conduct their relations on a basis of complete give and take. Neither party felt driven to calculate his rights and duties with respect to the other on a narrow contractual basis. As industrialisation proceeded, however, the employer increasingly imposed on the employee what the latter felt to be a low-trust pattern of work. That is to say, the employer chose less and less to rely on the employee's spirit of give and take, but sought the output or work performance he wanted by imposing more tightly defined, low-discretion job roles, programmed work sequences, closer supervision and harsher discipline. Yet while asserting a low-trust pattern over the employee, he hoped for a high-trust response in the form of willing compliance, loyalty and a ready confidence in his leadership.

THE EMPLOYEE RESPONSE

It was not forthcoming. Men respond to low trust with low trust. In an increasing number of situations, employees responded by withholding moral involvement in their employer's objectives, working indifferently and with little personal commitment, seeing the employer as pursuing his own interests to the exclusion of theirs, feeling used, therefore, in the service of goals not their own, manipulating the work situation for their benefit if opportunity permitted, practising restrictionism and obstructionism, organising themselves collectively, if they could, to force the employer to pay attention to their needs as well as his, and in general by refusing to conduct their relationship with him in the full spirit of high-trust problem-solving. Like him, they adopted the stance of contractual calculation. They preferred not to rely on his goodwill, if they could possibly avoid it, for what they sought from the employment relationship. Many of them, for much of the time, could not avoid it. Such is the meaning of weakness and dependence. But while the employer's power might be able to suppress open challenges, individual or collective, by his employees, it could not coerce them into willing loyalty and cooperation, for as we noted earlier such responses cannot be evoked by coercion.

Even as the new work patterns characteristic of Western industrialisation were emerging, therefore, they revealed features by no means to the liking of manufacturers and businessmen. Employees too often failed to offer the desired motivation and commitment, remaining alienated and increasingly showing signs of organising themselves against their masters. It is perhaps hardly necessary to add that only the occasional social observer traced their behaviour to their perceptions of those structural characteristics of the productive system which subjected them to low-discretion roles, minimal rewards and punitive discipline in order to serve the purposes of others. For the

E

55

most part employers avoided the uncomfortable implications of such an analysis much as they do still – by blaming the rank and file for their moral weakness, laziness, irresponsibility or sheer stupidity in being unable to grasp the economic facts of life.

Here and there were employers sufficiently motivated to seek ways of avoiding or minimising what for them were undesirable employee responses. In Britain this search was quickened by developments beginning in the closing decades of the nineteenth century. Competition from industrial rivals such as Germany and America made many manufacturers more sensitive to the costs of, and the yield from, their economic resources, of which labour was of course one. Trade unionism took a stride forward not only in industries and trades where it already had a secure foothold but also in many where it had not. Rising standards and mass education were stimulating the beginnings of that upward curve in rank-and-file aspirations which has continued ever since. Astute observers at all social levels were aware that irreversible changes were beginning to take place in the social position of labour – changes expressed also in the extension of the franchise to urban and rural wage-earners and in the recognition of poverty and deprivation as a social problem worthy of public discussion and calling for a public policy.

Within this total context two sets of ideas developed each of which claimed to offer employers a useful strategy for handling their labour in such ways as to overcome the potentially alienating effects of modern large-scale work organisation. One became known as Industrial Welfare, the other as Scientific Management.

EMPLOYER RESPONSES: INDUSTRIAL WELFARE

Sometimes referred to as 'betterment', the welfare approach concerned itself with such matters as the comfort, convenience and attractiveness of working conditions; providing cheap nourishing food in works canteens; appointing welfare supervisors to support and counsel employees in their personal problems; promoting social, sporting and cultural activities; and, in some cases, offering good low-cost housing for company workers along, perhaps, with other fringe benefits such as pensions and medical care. Some expressions of this approach embodied no more than a belief that the complex mechanism that is man works better and harder if tended with care. Here the strategy merged with what later became known as industrial psychology. In its beginnings this worked to a view of the individual as a machine needing careful study to establish the optimum conditions of its physical environment. Heating, lighting, ventilation, working hours and rest-pauses were all deemed relevant to individual fatigue and, by the same token, to the working efficiency of the human machine. Many welfare measures contained no rationale more subtle than this.

In some of its expressions, however, welfare was informed by a strategy of greater significance for our present analysis. This was no less than the search for a renewal of the reciprocal, diffuse bonds of obligation and loyalty believed to characterise earlier patterns of work organisation. If the employer manifested a concern for the interests and well-being of the employee – a concern for his physical, social and cultural welfare – would not the employee reciprocate with concern for the interests of the employer? Surely a demonstration by the latter of being ready to go beyond the narrow terms of the employment contract as ordinarily conceived would evoke a correspondingly generous response from the former? Thus would the stark cash-nexus that was generating such bitterness come to be enriched into a relationship of new depth in which the employee offered willing compliance, involvement and loyalty to his employer.

It was not difficult for the employer with this conception to become convinced that he was treating his employees as ends in themselves, rather than as means in an exploitative relationship. Yet all that the welfare movement really demonstrated was a conviction that self-interest on the part of the employer did not necessarily require that employees be treated harshly and inhumanely. If this was so then good management seemed to require that they be handled on generous and humane terms up to the point at which this policy was judged to be yielding diminishing returns. Short of this point, the employer – and even more his welfare manager or supervisor – might be able to assure himself of his moral virtue, which by definition was not yet being put to the test.

As we have seen, there had always been a few manufacturers

who tried, by paternalistic policies, to maintain a grateful and loyal labour force. Among them were Quakers like the Cadburys and Rowntrees, who were convinced that good morality was good business. Fair, humane and enlightened treatment of employees could not but benefit the company, it was felt, in the long if not necessarily the short run. And there were indeed situations where this seemed to be true, especially when the company appeared to face a prosperous expanding future. At a time when so many wage-earners were undernourished and overworked there might be economic advantages in a strategy which, by offering superior and genteel treatment, made it possible to select the most respectable applicants and promote their close attachment to the company by means of what, for the times, were considerate and humane terms of employment. That many aspects of this strategy were condescending and paternalist was of no consequence if the employees concerned accepted this view of their social status. No cynical calculation by such employers need be assumed. It was possible for a man with sincere religious convictions to want to succeed in business and to treat his employees kindly at the same time. If he were lucky he could do both, and it is naturally these happier coincidences which are likely to be recorded in the history of welfare. Many other employers, no doubt, would have liked to be kind but found their competitive circumstances such as to make them feel unable to afford such a luxury.

Even where they could, the welfare strategy was not necessarily successful. The greater the degree of conscious calculation which underlay it the more likely was such manipulative intent to show through and promote cynicism among the very people from whom it was designed to evoke trust. In any case, while welfare at its best might maintain a tolerably grateful, firmly attached labour force which thought well of the company – and such characteristics were not to be lightly dismissed – it could not seriously be expected to fulfil the more extravagant hopes entertained for it. Welfare policies were not the natural extension and reinforcement of a diffuse high-trust relationship developing between master and man as they worked alongside each other. They did not spring from a personalised relationship made possible by a simple division of labour and small-scale operations.

Had they done so they could indeed have knitted bonds of personal loyalty by expressing a concern which evoked a reciprocal commitment from the employee. Instead, welfare policies were an afterthought grafted on to the steely outlines of the modern bureaucratic work structure, within which rank-and-file employees, pursuing their highly subdivided, low-discretion roles, were subjected to elaborate mechanisms of supervision, inspection and control; were far removed from the centres of power, responsibility and important decision-making; and were conscious of being used for other men's purposes which they had no share in formulating. If company welfare policies convinced them that their employer was a considerate humane man of paternalistic benevolence they might prefer working for him – and be prepared to speak well of him. But to expect them to be significantly affected by these sentiments in the intensity of commitment with which they applied themselves to their anonymous, fragmented daily work routines was to misunderstand the nature of human motivation in work. Men can apply themselves freely and willingly to a task in either of two types of situation. The task itself may involve them as whole persons, calling upon a range and depth of their skills and qualities. Alternatively, though their task be a fragmented one they may be strongly committed to the end to which it is a contribution, feeling they are offering a willing involvement in a common purpose as against being used for the purposes of others. The modern work organisation provided too many of its rank-and-file employees with neither, and while welfare could both express and reinforce a relationship of reciprocal support which was generated and underpinned by one or other of these situations it could not by itself generate such a relationship in their absence. It could provide the icing on the cake, but it could not determine the quality of the cake itself.

In the event the welfare strategy offered little lasting satisfaction for either party. For employees, the gradual rise in living standards as the twentieth century progressed, along with a slow improvement in the standards of treatment offered by an increasing number of employers, served to reduce the relative superiority of the pioneer welfare companies. Moreover, welfare itself in the cultivated paternalist sense (as contrasted with simply being 'a good employer') was becoming less and less acceptable to its recipients. The heightened status of labour consequent on rising social respectability and aspirations, the increased coverage of trade unionism, an enlarged political role and the toehold of participation in governmental decision-making conceded during the First World War were rendering the paternalist concept outdated. The status implications of the father-child relationship, with the employees in tutelage to what the employer thought good for them, had begun to jar. Men started to wonder why they should not have the money value of welfare in their pay packet to spend how they liked – if necessary on a widening range of social and recreational facilities now increasingly available outside company boundaries.

These responses ensured that from the employers' point of view, too, welfare would never become a universal strategy even in its limited role of icing on the cake. Most of its practitioners soon decided that it did nothing significant to promote that unity of earnest endeavour which was the more ambitious purpose defined for it, and now even its lesser designs were showing diminishing returns. With the working week down to forty-eight hours, and with those lucky enough to have jobs usually receiving adequate nourishment by comparison with earlier times, there was less obvious return for the employer from policies designed to increase the physical efficiency of his human machines by tending them more carefully. Welfare, in short, was like any other resource available to management: it would be used insofar as management believed it to contribute in some fashion or another to managerial purposes, but would decline from favour as that belief became weakened or destroyed.

Recent years have seen some revival of the fundamental notion underlying welfare, this time focusing on the fringe symbols of status. The first step in this approach is to draw attention to the persistent differences of treatment, sometimes as between manual and non-manual employees, sometimes as between higher salary-earners on the one hand and wage-earning and lower salary-earning employees on the other, in such respects as pensions, sick pay, holidays, clocking-in, canteen facilities and various other fringe characteristics of the work situation. These status differences of treatment are then related to differences in the degree to which the respective groups are integrated into the organisation in the moral involvement sense. The observation that superior status treatment along the dimensions of these fringe characteristics is usually accompanied by greater moral involvement is then presumed to have direct causal implications. If lower-rank groups can be assimilated to the higher-rank groups in respect of these treatments, perhaps this elevation in terms of status will evoke an equivalent elevation in terms of moral involvement? Some companies are accordingly introducing schemes of 'staff status' for all or selected categories of lower-rank employees.

Such schemes are sometimes but one element in a wider programme which can include other organisational changes such as the redefinition of jobs and the restructuring of supervision, so there would be difficulty in gauging the effects of so-called staff status alone. There is reason to believe, however, that like many other strategies in this field the staff status approach by itself is notable more for its hopefulness than its logic. To suppose that the greater involvement of higher-rank employees derives significantly from superior treatment in these fringe characteristics reveals the same neglect of the more fundamental differences in work situation that we noted in the earlier welfare approach. There is no cause to doubt that manual workers offered tangible improvements in their terms of employment, such as pensions and sick pay, will grasp them with alacrity and may feel a stronger attachment to the company if these features distinguish it from others. And management may be seeking no more than this. But there is little sign that workers read into such changes a degree of symbolic status significance sufficient to elevate their moral involvement in the company to a significantly higher level. Far more basic changes than this are likely to be required – changes in discretion, responsibility, autonomy, sense of individuality of contribution, consciousness of membership of the high-trust fraternity. Possibly the only significant consequence for top management of equalising fringe benefits and status symbols may prove to be a sense of grievance among some white-collar groups at losing the consciousness of privilege which they derived from these traditional superior benefits. Combined with other tendencies such as the depersonalisation and intensified routinisation observable in certain white-collar situations, this could contribute to a net loss of moral involvement.

Thus welfare is no more likely in its current manifestations than in its earlier forms to offer a major contribution to the twin problems of management we are concerned with here – namely, how to promote willing employee compliance with management's rules, policies and leadership, and how perhaps to go beyond that to generate a positive, active involvement and identification with management's values and purposes. If welfare could not fill this bill, still less could the other set of ideas with which we are concerned in this chapter, namely those underlying Scientific Management.

EMPLOYER RESPONSES: SCIENTIFIC MANAGEMENT

At first sight there may seem cause for surprise that Scientific Management could be conceived by anybody as a possible basis for willing employee compliance and moral involvement. The reason for surprise is evident when we recall the practical techniques with which it is usually associated. Time and motion study, piecework and bonus payment systems, cost accounting methods and a wide range of other efficiency devices – these are redolent of a view of labour as needing to be programmed, graded and dragooned rather than as a potentially eager and willing partner in a common enterprise. Yet underlying the efficiency techniques of Frederick Taylor and the other Scientific Management pioneers was a philosophy which they saw as ushering in a state of industrial harmony, fruitful cooperation and mutual advantage if only employers and employees could be persuaded to break with the attitudes so often generated by industrialism. These can be summed up – to recall the terminology used in the previous chapter – as those of a win-lose game. In Taylor's view, employers and employees too often adopted towards each other a stance of opposition and conflict – the former acting on an assumption that low labour costs required low wages, and the latter, similarly, that pursuit of their own interests required 'victory' in a struggle against the employer. Within the context of these mutually impoverishing sets of attitudes, employers practised unscientific rule-of-thumb methods and imposed arbitrary dictatorial government on employees, while the latter responded with uncooperativeness and restrictionism.

Taylor's solution called for a complete 'mental revolution' on both sides. In place of the mutually-antagonistic win-lose attitudes, they were to adopt what was referred to earlier as a problem-solving approach to their joint relations. They must grasp the fact that if they dropped their hostile defences in favour of full collaboration they could between them so enlarge the total product that the fight about shares would be transcended in the knowledge that there was ample wealth for all. This 'mental revolution' was the essence of Scientific Management for Taylor, who went out of his way to insist that it:

> is not a new system of figuring costs; it is not a new system of paying men; it is not a piece-work system; it is not a bonus system; it is not a premium system; it is no scheme for paying men; it is not holding a stopwatch on a man and writing things down about him; it is not time study; it is not motion study nor an analysis of the movements of men . . . it is not any of the devices which the average man calls to mind when scientific management is spoken of.

Rather was it an appeal to management and men to join in a unity of purpose on the basis of 'economic man' – on the basis, that is, of maximising financial reward. To be sure, the description of Taylor's vision as a problem-solving situation might seem to some extent a misnomer, for he planned no creative role for labour in his proposed scientific transformation of work methods. Taylor's opinion of the rank-and-file employee was unflattering. Most men were naturally lazy, evasive of responsibilities and of limited ability. They had to be motivated by the external goads of the carrot and stick – by financial incentives and punishments. But motivated along what patterns of work behaviour? These were to be programmed by the minority elite of planners, thinkers and analysts who were capable of self-motivation and self-control. They were to design the best methods and impose them on the rank and file. The proper destiny for labour was to seek maximum money rewards by submitting to scientifically-designed work systems and incentives devised by the elite.

Yet a problem-solving spirit among employees could by no means be dispensed with even under this arrangement. For smooth and fruitful working it required employees to offer a

willing and cooperative recognition of the job rules and programmes laid down for them – a recognition which derived
from acceptance that these were the best rules discoverable for
serving their own interests as well as management's. In other
words, the problem-solving spirit was implicit in this very readiness to accept work methods which aimed supposedly at promoting the joint advantage of employer and employee. The
suspicious obstructionism, wary manœuvring and bargaining
gamesmanship characteristic of the win-lose approach were to
be dropped in favour of the trusting receptiveness, flexibility
and open communications of the problem-solving scene. The
employer also, of course, had adjustments to make. His contribution was that he, too, had to submit to the scientific designs of
the work engineers and planners. He had, moreover, to rid
himself of any notion that his advantage required employees to
be disadvantaged. He had to work to the assumptions that he
pursued his own interests best by maximising the employees'
opportunities to pursue theirs, and that what they sought to
maximise was financial reward. On this basis would rest a
mutuality of interest that guaranteed industrial harmony and
ensured full employee cooperation.

Both parties disappointed Taylor's hopes. Employers and
managers were apt to resent the pretensions of the Scientific
Management school to supersede their authority, prerogatives
and judgement with the dictates of professional specialists. Even
greater was the failure of employees to lend themselves willingly
to these purposes. Where strong enough they resisted the application of the stopwatch, the analysis of work, its detailed break-
down into fragmented tasks, and indeed the whole drive towards
precise measurement and heightened control. They showed
themselves utterly unready to offer commitment to Taylor's
philosophy of a mutuality of interest. Often they were compelled, through weakness, to submit to certain dictates with
respect to their work routines. But this was forced, not willing,
compliance, and where possible they evaded the rules or mani-
pulated them to serve their own needs. Thus was aggravated a
battle of wits between controllers and controlled which continues to the present day.

Why did employees in general feel unable to accept the
Scientific Management invitation to join, in a problem-solving

spirit, a common effort to maximise productive efficiency? The brief answer is that they felt unable to return a high-trust response to what they perceived as a low-trust situation. This calls for some elaboration. We have already characterised the problem-solving relationship as a high-trust relationship in which men work to an assumption of common goals, communicate freely and without calculation, refrain from the gamesmanship of the win-lose approach, and work through their disagreements by rational discussion instead of taking up a conflict bargaining stance. But we have also seen that such a pattern of behaviour is unlikely to prevail among rank-and-file members of industrial societies marked by extreme division of labour, acquisitive values, and some freedom to formulate and act on ideologies which challenge managerial prerogative. Their fragmented jobs, their remoteness from important decision-making, and their sense of being subordinated to other men's purposes prompt them to define their interests as in some respects divergent from management's. But this is simply another way of saying they feel unable wholly to trust management. They have no confidence that management will govern in ways which fully serve their needs and interests. It is for this reason that they seek to change the decision-making process – either by unilaterally imposing their own rules and decisions, by securing their interests through legislation, or by bringing pressure to bear on management in a process of bilateral or joint regulation.

When we examine the Scientific Management vision in this context we see how improbable it was. Employees were expected to cooperate constructively with management and to take on trust that in the unspecified future management would allocate them certain unspecified rewards which would prove to meet their aspirations. This is precisely the sort of open-ended high-trust commitment which low-discretion employees in large-scale organisations feel unable to make. Taylor and his supporters were naive also in their assumption that with respect to rewards men are concerned only with 'more'. For men are concerned also with justice – which means they compare their own rewards with those received by others. Most of us are interested in justice only in a 'particularist' sense – that is to say, in justice for ourselves and our group – rather than in a

65

'universalist' sense – namely in a system which seeks justice for everybody. Nevertheless justice is a potent force in that many disputes which, on the face of it, are about money are in fact about 'fairness', and employees invited to cooperate freely with management and 'trust the company' frequently feel unable to rely on diffuse (unspecified) promises. Only when management has accompanied the invitation with the offer of specifically-guaranteed shares in the increased production expected to result (as with comprehensive productivity agreements) have organised work-groups and unions been prepared to extend the desired collaboration, and then only on a rigorously defined basis.

Thus the Scientific Management vision failed to materialise. The notion of the work organisation as a high-trust, problem-solving corporate team, pursuing wealth in the confident expectation of meeting no problems about its distribution, foundered on the fact that in the eyes of its rank-and-file participants the organisation was no high-trust team in that sense. Whatever management might *say* about teamwork and trust, its *behaviour* suggested to them a very different set of attitudes. By the very act of subjecting them to tightly prescribed work roles, excluding them from the important decision-making, and allocating them greatly inferior rewards, status and respect, it implied that it saw them as means to be used towards its own ends. And increasingly the rank and file were combining to return low trust with low trust. Just as management showed, by defining them as inferiors, that it did not propose to trust them, so they reciprocated by distrusting management and seeking to bind it to observe certain terms and conditions of employment, to refrain from arbitrary rule, and to concede limited rights of appeal against certain types of decision.

In such a context as this, Scientific Management techniques could only aggravate distrust. Within a high-trust group pursuing common goals, its methods of systematic investigation, analysis and work programming could be welcomed by all as promoting efficiency. Within a low-trust group where goals were divergent, subordinates saw them as intensified manifestations by superiors of distrust and manipulative intent. Perceived as such, they could never serve as jointly-legitimised means towards jointly-legitimised ends. Instead they became, for many employees, symbols of the intensified exploitation of their labour.

The managerial search for that unity of purpose which would generate willing compliance and positive motivation therefore had to take a different path. There was little sign that such unity could be built on an appeal to 'economic' man. By the 1940s a new hope had appeared. Perhaps it could be built on the concept of 'social' man? The Human Relations vogue, to which we now turn, was soon in full swing among that small minority of companies receptive to new ideas in the emerging field of 'man-management'.

Further Reading

BRIGGS, A. *Seebohm Rowntree*. London: Longmans, 1961.

HABER, S. *Efficiency and Uplift: Scientific Management in the Progressive Era 1890–1920*. Chicago: University of Chicago Press, 1964.

INGHAM, G. *Size of Industrial Organization and Worker Behaviour*. Cambridge: At the University Press, 1970.

TILLETT, A., KEMPNER, T., WILLS, G. *Management Thinkers*. Harmondsworth: Penguin Books, 1970.

4. Consent and 'Social' versus 'Economic' Man

Taylor's vision had contained the notion of an appeal to the individual employee to offer willing compliance with 'scientific' job-designers and work planners so that wealth could be maximised in the interests of all. Aware of collective efforts among employees to pursue restrictionism, obstructionism and other modes of challenge, he hoped they could be induced to forswear such behaviours in the pursuit of a larger joint purpose with management. But as we have seen, this was tantamount to inviting them to offer high-trust responses to what they saw as a low-trust situation created and imposed by management. Extreme division of labour, rigorous subordination, the use of superior economic power to hire, discipline and fire the lower orders, their exclusion from higher decision-making – such features constituted for the rank and file a pattern of low-trust relations to which they could only respond with low-trust behaviours of their own. Whatever the 'mutuality of interests' vision cherished by Taylor, management saw the techniques of Scientific Management simply as devices for utilising labour resources more efficiently in the service of its own ends. This only confirmed the employee consciousness of being used to serve the purposes of others.

Taylor was neither the first nor the last to be keenly aware of these low-trust responses by employees but to offer no acknowledgement whatever that they were evoked by employee perceptions of the basic structural features of the work organisation and of the society in which it was embedded. He pressed his formula in the apparent belief that the responses could be fundamentally changed without changing the social and industrial structures which evoked them. We noted in the preceding chapter that the same belief had been held by some exponents of the industrial welfare approach. In their case it took the form of supposing that an organised, institutionalised expression of concern for the employee's welfare beyond the stark contractual cash nexus would evoke from him an equivalent concern for the interests of management. In Taylor's case an exhortation to both sides to substitute problem-solving for win-lose attitudes was the method chosen. In neither was there acknowledgement that the widespread incidence of win-lose attitudes on both sides sprang not from a wilful and foolish choice of the 'wrong' sentiments but from constraints, pressures and values generated by the social and economic system itself. The same neglect of basic structure was to be a feature of the early Human Relations approach soon to be examined.

It is no hard task to locate the reasons for this marked disinclination to look deep for explanations of alienated indifference and sometimes militant hostility in the responses of employees to management rule. For employers, managers and others enjoying power, high rewards, high status and high job discretion, the structural characteristics of industrial society were proving very acceptable. Large hierarchical organisations, division of labour and mechanisation were producing great wealth and expanding opportunities for the clever, the lucky and the ruthless. Even a critical observer might accept too that, as a by-product of the process, the position of many others was improved. While the greater proportion of the population had little or no real choice in determining either the ends pursued by the economic system or the means employed to serve those ends, certain benefits in respect of living standards were filtering down which they could be presumed to welcome. Among men of power and influence, therefore, few were likely to feel driven to turn a searching eye upon the system which favoured them, and to see its basic features as responsible for the responses, at best often lack-lustre, at worst alienated and hostile, of rank-and-file employees. Less disturbing and more convenient was to see these responses as caused by foolishness, moral weakness or subversive agitators, and as being curable by managerial action, attitudinal changes or marginal modifications in the work situation which left the fundamental features of the structure intact.

SOCIAL MAN AND THE HUMAN RELATIONS APPROACH

It is with these considerations in mind that we turn to examine the Human Relations approach. Taylor's hope of conjuring away the collective employee challenges and obstructions to management rule remained only a dream, but this very capacity among workers for group sentiment, cohesion and action was to prove the vehicle of the next managerial strategy for seeking employee involvement without essentially changing the system. It had been evident for a long time that employee work-groups could evolve their own norms and values and thereby strongly influence the attitudes and behaviour of their individual members. Craft custom and practice among groups of skilled apprenticed men constituted a painfully familiar example for some employers. Some of the attitudes and work rules imposed by the group culture upon the members might benefit management, but there were many which it found restrictive and irksome. For the most part, in fact, group control of this kind was a tiresome constraint upon management, for its purpose was to defend earnings, job security, craft skills and group cohesion against threats presented by management in the course of pursuing its own goals. Sooner or later, however, the notion was likely to emerge that the ability of group norms and values to influence individual attitudes and behaviour was a resource which management could turn to its advantage. At present the informal leadership and norms of such groups were often such as ran counter to top management objectives and policies. But what if management could divert the leadership and allegiance of these informal work groups into its own hands? Norms and values could then be introduced into the group culture which favoured management's purposes. The springs of human motivation, loyalty and involvement which at present were so often directed along oppositional channels would be harnessed to serve management ends.

But how was this to be done? For one prominent group of researchers and theorists the answer was suggested by their explanation of why employees formed informal groups in the first place. The explanation was in terms not of 'economic' man but of 'social' man. It was argued that industrialism and urbanism were destroying the small, close-knit, traditional communities within which every man had an acknowledged place and function, saw that his function, however humble, had meaning for his group, drew identity and recognition from his discharge of it, and derived satisfaction from his participation in the group's purpose. These, it was argued, were basic social needs felt by all men even more keenly than their economic needs. Yet these social needs were being ignored in modern work organisations. Management, in failing to direct planned effort towards the creation of the right social conditions of work, was denying employees all sense of identity, of belonging, and of participation in a group or community purpose. Since men cannot long endure this atomised and isolated state they try to meet their social needs by forging informal group links, acknowledging informal group leaders, and evolving informal group norms and values. Since this structure is developed by employees themselves out of frustration at management's neglect of their needs, it was likely to be oriented towards opposition to management. Hence the diversion of energy, commitment and loyalty to purposes divergent from management's.

The desirable strategy thus seemed to be apparent. Management itself must meet these social needs in a consciously organised manner and recruit group affiliations for its own ends. Managerial leadership must be substituted for informal (and potentially subversive) leadership by training managers in the arts and skills of winning men's allegiance. Such leadership skills were specially important for first-line supervisors and foremen, for these were in close daily contact with rank-and-file work-groups. Included in these so-called 'social skills' were the ability to extend sympathetic consideration to employee needs and feelings, to offer supportive and consultative rather than punitive supervision, to promote in the individual a sense of group belonging and identity by recognising him as a person with a contribution to make, to invite cooperation rather than extort obedience, and to promote a sense of group purpose in which all could participate. With the members of the work-group now turning to him as their leader and offering him that spirit of commitment and identification which all men need and want to offer, the manager could use that spirit as a resource in the service of managerial ends. Such, briefly stated, was the

F

essence of the Human Relations message for management. Properly and imaginatively interpreted and applied, such a strategy could, it was felt, construct for the atomised and isolated individuals of industrial society a social context at the workplace within which they could reknit the social bonds they needed and live satisfying lives. Thus could management both serve its own interests and strengthen the social fabric at the same time by consciously planning for a healthy harmony and common purpose, rather than allowing their organisations to drift by default into disharmony and unhealthy conflict.

This could seem an attractive message even for those with no direct axe to grind. For those few managers interested enough to listen it could seem a very attractive message indeed. Like the grander versions of industrial welfare and Scientific Management, it held out the picture of a unity of purpose which might still be recoverable from the hatreds and prejudices into which the work organisation had fallen. These were due to management not yet having realised that willing cooperation in the conditions of modern industry could not be left to chance, on the assumption that it would emerge spontaneously. It had to be actively promoted, and this required special management skills. All these skills required, by their very nature, to be exercised through communication with others. Projecting a democratic, supportive and consultative leadership, transmitting sympathetic consideration towards employee needs and feelings, expounding aims and purposes in a manner designed to evoke active cooperation from others, conducting processes of working through disagreements in such a way as to clarify the common purpose while elucidating the errors of fact or reasoning which had created the disagreements – all these called for careful cultivation of the skills of human communication. Thus it became – and in many quarters remains – fashionable to argue that the frictions and apparent conflicts to be found in industry were essentially caused by failures of communication. Management had not sufficiently developed its social skills. The special sin of trade unions was that, given management's default, they exploited these communication failures by deliberately organising employees in a conflict stance, thereby rendering more elusive the spirit of shared purpose which nevertheless still remained within reach given management will and ability.

Here, then, was a doctrine of good cheer for management. Admittedly its opening proposition might not seem to fit that description. The emphasis on informal group norms and values as the major determinants of individual attitudes and behaviour implied that the management-designed formal structure, with its rules, controls and incentives, was of lesser consequence. And indeed one result of the Human Relations approach was a concentration of research and theorising upon small-group dynamics rather than upon the effects on behaviour of such formal aspects as technology, work-flow, control systems and pay structures, and their interaction with the organisation's environment and wider social setting. Yet, though this opening proposition might seem initially lowering, the gloom could be quickly dispelled with the assurance that given cultivation of the right skills management could capture leadership of the informal groups. Reinforcement was also offered, for those managers who wanted it, to the notion that trade unions were essentially mischievous agencies with an institutional interest in sowing and aggravating distrust. But accompanying this reinforcement was the implication that they could be kept at bay provided management applied the necessary arts to evoke the willing participation and identification which, in their hearts, all men needed and wanted to give. Conflict was a symptom of faulty management styles, not of deep-seated perceptions by employees of divergent interest as between themselves and management. The central message which seemed to emerge from the whole approach, therefore, was that the arts and crafts of man-management as commended by the Human Relations approach constituted the most important determinant of employee behaviour.

Such were the attractions of this doctrine for managers and others concerned to strengthen and facilitate the smooth working of the *status quo* that there need be no surprise either at its having been evolved in the first place or at its eager reception among those managements alert to such messages. The appeal remains today. Management's response to it, however, is now more likely to be wistful than hopeful, for it cannot be said to have proved itself in the dusty arena of the business enterprise. Exploring the reasons for its failure will occupy us for the rest of this chapter. In the process we shall find ourselves noting a wide diversity of other influences besides management's social skills which shape men's attitudes and behaviour at work.

The first step in our critical examination of the Human Relations approach is to note the fallacy at the heart of it. Its theorists singled out for special attention the fact that employees showed a marked tendency to relate themselves to each other in informal groups whose culture then greatly influenced their individual behaviour. In answer to the question 'why?' they explained these spontaneous group affiliations in terms of men's social needs. Employees came together in this way because they wanted the satisfactions and the sense of identity and belonging which could be derived from group membership and participation. The significance of this type of explanation was crucial. For if the objectives which men pursued through their involvement in groups were simply the *intrinsic* satisfactions of membership and participation, then by definition they might find one type of group goal as acceptable as any other. The vital condition for them would be that they involved themselves in a community of endeavour, and the exact nature of the endeavour might not be all that important.

The implications for the informal work-group are plain to see. The Human Relations theorists had noted that it was often oriented in opposition to management goals. But if the essential satisfactions for members derived not from the fact of the group pursuing anti-management goals but simply from the fact of being integrated into a group *per se*, then the group could be oriented to pursue pro-management goals without loss to its members. They would gain the same satisfactions from the latter situation as from the former. Provided management could offer them the same experience of group involvement, they would be as ready to follow pro-management as anti-management leadership.

If, on the other hand, the primary reason why men came together in groups was not to secure the *intrinsic* satisfactions derivable from membership, but to combine in order the more effectively to pursue certain *extrinsic* objectives, then the foregoing chain of reasoning collapses. The group would then be seen by its members predominantly as a means to certain specific ends. To be sure, members might also derive intrinsic satisfactions from their mutual cooperation, trust and fellowship which they would be sorry to lose, but these would not be the reasons why the group evolved. The basis of group affiliation would therefore be totally different from that postulated by the early Human Relations school, which envisaged members valuing the group not as a means to an end, but as an end in itself. If, then, cohesive work-groups with their own norms and values developed, not to bring their members intrinsic social satisfactions, but to secure certain of their extrinsic economic interests against management rules, policies and decisions (or indeed against threats from other work-groups), any management hope of winning the groups' allegiance was bound to seem forlorn.

Such a line of argument was disagreeable to the early Human Relations theorists. It suggested that the structural conditions of the business enterprise were such as to generate employee perceptions of certain divergent interests which might not easily be dispelled by management's social skills and sophisticated communications techniques. It drew attention to the conflict aspects of management/worker relations, whereas they preferred to stress the underlying harmony which they thought could be revealed by the correct managerial style. More congenial to them in the light of this preference was the belief that men pursue involvement in the informal work-group for the sake of its intrinsic satisfactions, not for any extrinsic goals.

The argument of this book has, of course, been that given the structural nature of the enterprise, and given the probable orientations and aspirations of its members, along with the institutions and values of the society in which it is embedded, low-trust relations are likely to prevail. Management's imposition of detailed subordination and control is likely to be reciprocated by employee suspicion and often collective resistance. Managerial attempts to persuade employees to comply willingly in the interests of a common purpose have often foundered on the employees' experience that their welfare would be considered only insofar as this served, at best, management's enlightened, long-term interests, at worst a ruthless pursuit of short-term profit. Accordingly they have, where possible, frequently drawn together into cohesive groups and trade unions and, to the extent they felt necessary, resisted or obstructed management rule covertly or overtly in attempts to defend themselves within their work environment. If we apply this analysis to the Human Relations approach it leads to the proposition that the primary impulse behind informal group structure, insofar as its members evolve norms and values which run counter to management purposes, is to pursue the extrinsic goals of defending and advancing their job interests as they see them. Thus management is unable to rally such groups to its support by the techniques of Human Relations, since they spring from a distrust of management which they naturally turn upon the Human Relations techniques themselves.

So management continued to be faced with the same array of employee responses as before, for while, as always, exceptions were to be found, the return on these techniques was at best small and temporary. Meanwhile, in the postwar period, research increasingly documented a wide diversity of factors which could bear upon the perceptions of employees so as to shape their attitudes, the nature and degree of their grievances and resentments, and their manner of expressing them. This evidence seriously damaged the Human Relations notion that the nature and quality of management/worker relations depended primarily on management's skills in meeting employees' social needs (as this approach defined them). Increasingly apparent was the fact that work-group behaviour might be shaped by many other influences besides management's social skills. Indeed this much could be deduced simply from the observation that informal group behaviour was often strongly oriented not towards social needs but towards economic and job needs. This meant that all those factors affecting their economic and job interests, including not only those internal to the enterprise with their roots in organisational design and company policy, but also many which were external to the enterprise, might be relevant in explaining why employee groups behaved as they did. No outside observer of a particular enterprise at a particular time could explain its members' behaviour without detailed empirical inquiry, but he could be helped in making such an inquiry by knowing what lines of investigation it would be sensible to pursue.

EMPLOYEE PERCEPTIONS AND THEIR EXTERNAL
DETERMINANTS

Reference was made in the preceding paragraph to factors
bearing upon the perceptions of employees. The notion of perceptions is so crucial as to need a little elaboration before we
explore the structural influences of enterprise and society upon
work behaviour. A beginning would be to note the obvious fact
that observers wearing differently coloured spectacles see the
same view in different terms. If we substitute for the spectacles
the notion of a frame of reference which is a distillation of the
observer's background, experience, values and purposes, the
reason is soon apparent why, when we try to understand his
responses, we must remember that they arise from *his* perceptions of the situation, not our own. A work-group on a mass-
production assembly line whose members have abandoned any
aim they may have had of intrinsically satisfying work and who
seek only to maximise earnings will conduct itself differently
from one whose members would be ready to sacrifice some
money in exchange for a more interesting job. This means that
bound up with the question of so-called 'structural determinants
of behaviour' of the sort we are about to examine is the question
of how people perceive these structural features, since how they
perceive them decides how they behave in response.

The elements which contribute to the individual's frame of
reference are many and diverse. Some of them have behavioural
implications which are not too difficult to predict. If men's
experiences at the hands of family, school, friends, job and the
mass media sharpen their aspirations for a rising material
standard of life but do not encourage a search for intrinsic
satisfactions in work, there need be no surprise if they become
specially aggressive and competitive about money rewards at
the expense of other kinds. If their present standard of life is
dependent upon remaining in work they can be expected to
resist, if they can, being rendered unemployed. Societies with a
strong cultural tradition of deference to officially-constituted
authority offer a more favourable environment for managers in
certain vital respects than do societies where attitudes are less
respectful.

When men enter an organisation they bring with them

values on a wide variety of such matters, though of course the values may be changed by their experience within it. There are many other possible external influences. Employee behaviour in terms of turnover, absence, sickness and other forms which can often be expressions of discontent may be affected by the availability or otherwise of suitable alternative jobs. Some local communities have a tradition of militancy and hostility towards employers; others a tradition of accommodation and peace. Government action on, for example, labour legislation, incomes, taxation and rents can sometimes affect union or work-group strike behaviour or wages policy whatever management may or may not do. Trade unions to which the employees belong may have national or district policies, traditions, characters or styles which affect either favourably or unfavourably their members' receptivity of management initiatives.

All these are examples of external factors which can shape the values, attitudes and behaviour of the groups which the Human Relations manager tries to woo for his own purposes. Already it becomes evident that even these could be sufficiently potent in some cases to become the major determinant of work-group action. Such influences as he brings to bear on their behaviour through the arts and crafts of Human Relations man-management might easily be swamped by other, more powerful forces shaping their responses. The case becomes even clearer when we add to these external influences a range of structural features *within* the organisation. It is then apparent that work situations vary widely in the extent to which employee behaviour is susceptible to managerial modification by social skills alone. Some may be highly so, others not at all, and since the outsider with no special knowledge cannot predict a given situation in advance the manager is dependent in his choice of strategy upon an informed analysis of his own particular case.

EMPLOYEE PERCEPTIONS AND THEIR INTERNAL DETERMINANTS

Of major importance among these internal factors are technology, job design, work-flow, control systems and other structural characteristics of the productive system. Differences in these features are often accompanied by differences in the attitudes and behaviour of the job occupants. This can be illustrated by comparing two familiar occupational categories, the unskilled machine-operator and the research scientist. The former, occupying a low-status, low-discretion, subordinate role closely circumscribed by rules and controls, is likely to display little or no moral involvement with job or organisation. He may draw a sharp line between work and leisure, measure his contribution with grudging calculation, and generally distrust management as much as he perceives management distrusting him. The latter, occupying a high-status, high-discretion superior role, is more likely to display moral involvement with his work, feel that it expresses him as much as, possibly more than, do his leisure activities, offer himself to it freely and without stint, and be conscious of a measure of fraternity with seniors and superiors.

The importance of the employee's frame of reference should remind us always to bring into our analysis the external influences already mentioned which help to shape it and therefore help to shape his responses to the work situation. The attitudinal and behavioural differences we have noted are not to be explained solely in terms of objective facts about the two job situations. Each, before he takes up his job, is likely, in the manner noted in the first chapter, to have come under educational, subcultural and family influences whose effects are to prepare him for his work role by encouraging an appropriate set of attitudes. The machine-operator-to-be, as he moves through his secondary modern school, picking up clues about society and his probable place in it from family, newspaper and television, and exchanging impressions with his friends and peers, is likely to form expectations that work will be a dull and largely frustrating subordination to the mysterious and uncontrollable purposes of others, with the pay packet as its most important meaning and purpose. The research scientist, passing through private or grammar school and university, will more probably learn the very different set of expectations that he will make serious, considered choices about something called a career, which will have a central meaning and purpose in his life, will develop, stretch and challenge him as a person, and will yield him both extrinsic and intrinsic rewards.

These learned attitudes enter into the frame of reference

through which each perceives his work role and its surrounding social context. But it is also apparent that neither would be able to express these learned attitudes and manifest the learned behaviour unless the nature and conditions of his job situation made this possible. It is the job situation itself that confirms expectations and assumptions about what sorts of attitudes and behaviour are appropriate. Sometimes, of course, men come to their job with an inappropriate set of expectations. Perhaps the adolescent taking up his role as machine-operator imagines that the adult world of work will give him status, stimulus and interest. Perhaps the research scientist is unprepared for the life of diffuse commitment and moral involvement he is expected to offer, preferring the more specific and structured demands of a nine-to-five routine. Both, in the long run, will have to adapt, either by (a) cultivating a more congruent frame of reference or (b) searching for a work situation more congruent with his existing expectations or (c) modifying – if he can – his present work situation and what it requires of him. The importance of the job itself is therefore evident in confirming certain attitudes, behaviours and aspirations, and discouraging others.

The contrast just drawn was a sharp and obvious one between the high-discretion, high-status professional world and that of the low-discretion, low-status, rank-and-file job. But even within the world of the rank and file there are diversities of job situation which evoke significant variations of attitude and behaviour. Some of these, too, are obvious enough, such as those between, on the one hand, the coalminer, the deepsea fisherman or the shipbuilding craftsman, and on the other hand the stores clerk, the part-time married woman operative and the engineering apprentice aspiring to become a draughtsman. One line of research, which proved somewhat embarrassing for the Human Relations emphasis on face-to-face social skills and supervisory and communications techniques as the primary determinants of employee behaviour, discovered a measure of consistency in the similarities and differences of strike behaviour among a range of industries in different countries. Only the briefest indication of the results can be given here, and it must suffice to say that certain industries appeared to be relatively strike-prone wherever they were found, while others appeared relatively strike-free. A comparison, for example, of Western

Europe, the United States, Australia and New Zealand, showed mining and the docks demonstrating a high propensity for strike behaviour, and railways and agriculture a low propensity, with chemicals, printing and leather coming somewhere in between. While both the collection and interpretation of such data are complex and controversial activities needing extreme wariness and occasioning keen debate, one point seems incontrovertible for our immediate purposes: any consistent differences between industries above the level of mere chance confirm the inadequacy of the Human Relations nostra. The assertion that the nature of management/worker relations depends upon the Human Relations skills of management would seem to require us to believe that, whereas in railways and agriculture throughout all the relevant countries managers happened to be well endowed with these skills, those in the mining and docks industries chanced, by an equally curious coincidence, to be devoid of them. This can hardly be included among the more plausible explanations of such differences.

Important differences of attitude and behaviour remain even when we contract our focus from these inter-industrial comparisons to those likely to be found within, say, any large engineering plant. One piece of research points to work-group differences which could easily be found coexisting within such a plant, though the researcher's findings were in fact drawn from a study of three hundred groups spread over a wide range of manufacturing industry. His results led him to differentiate groups into four broad categories marked by distinct differences of behaviour – the Apathetic, Erratic, Strategic and Conservative.

Apathetic groups were unlikely to challenge management decisions or, for that matter, those of their union leaders. They advanced few grievances and used pressure tactics little. They had no clearly identified leaders and suffered internal disunity. But although they revealed little effective capacity to organise and express their grievances there were often signs of suppressed discontent among them. Such groups tended to be relatively low-skilled and low-paid, and were often found in departments where each worker performed a different function using distinctive equipment – mixed departments, in other words, where the common elements between jobs were limited, and likewise the incentive for group action.

Erratic groups were unstable, highly demonstrative and volatile in their behaviour, revealing little apparent relation between the severity of their grievance and the intensity of their protest. They were easily aroused, often inconsistent, and occasioned management more than the usual difficulty in predicting their reactions. Their members were engaged on identical or nearly identical tasks, were often required to interact with each other, and performed operations which were primarily worker-controlled as distinct from machine-controlled.

Strategic groups maintained continuous pressure on management in pursuit of their self-interests, planned their grievance activities carefully, enjoyed a high degree of internal unity, and played a strong part in the running of the union. Most of the jobs involved consisted of individual operations rather than being technologically interdependent as in the case of the erratic groups. They were somewhat superior to those of the two preceding categories – not the best jobs in the plant but in the middle of the range. The skills required often called for a certain amount of personal judgement and were often seen by management as important.

Finally, the Conservative groups, which were the most stable, were also the most self-assured and successful. They rarely had grievances, but when they went into action did so calmly and unhurriedly. Somewhat self-sufficient, they were less likely than strategic groups to participate in union affairs. Their jobs were to be found at the top of both the status and promotional ladders so far as manual work was concerned, and enjoyed a monopoly of scarce skills deemed very important in the plant. Most of their work consisted of individual operations, but sometimes several would be found working together in a repair or maintenance crew.

Such is a brief indication of one body of research into work-group behaviour. It concerns American experience, and reference to it here is intended not necessarily to support either the particular classifications suggested or the particular structural analysis put forward to explain them, but to illustrate one approach to the understanding of work situations which provides an indispensable supplement to the Human Relations emphasis. That emphasis was that employee behaviour, influenced as it is by group membership, could be brought, by means of a planned strategy of Human Relations skills with respect to supervisory styles, communications techniques and the arts of personal leadership, to support management policies and objectives. Supplementing this as a consequence of postwar research was now the structural emphasis which alerted management to the possibility that the behaviour of work-groups might be determined, not by management's Human Relations skills, but by group perceptions of, and reactions to, technological and engineering factors, work-flow arrangements and other characteristics of the division of labour in the plant. And it is a major theme of this book that these perceptions and reactions often lead to a wary, low-trust stance which is not susceptible of being changed simply by management leadership, manipulative supervision and communications skills.

This is not to deny that the personality factors and interpersonal relations emphasised by Human Relations can be important in some situations. Indeed, in the analysis just examined it was a characteristic of groups in the Apathetic and Erratic categories that they tended to seek out and respond positively to active leadership, and their behaviour could change according to the nature of the leadership offered. Were it highly aggressive in nature the group could develop hostile relations with management (or union), but a change of leader could bring about rapid conversion to a more accommodating pattern. Such groups, unlike the Strategic and Conservative varieties, might be thought to be open to the sort of manipulation proposed by the Human Relations strategy, which would seek to establish a leadership favourable to management. Other research, too, showed that some groups seemed, as a consequence of the very nature of their work situation and job arrangements, to be cooperatively disposed.

This research might seem to suggest, then, that if (a) by their very structural nature, certain types of work-group respond and behave more conveniently for management than do others, and (b) the nature of a group is to some extent shaped by technological factors, the division of labour, and the way work is organised, this knowledge could be consciously exploited by management for its own benefit. Perhaps jobs and work arrangements could be so designed as to create more cooperative and amenable work-groups? Our analysis enables us to identify a major flaw, however, in this strategy. Work-group behaviour is not a simple and direct reflection of the objective work situation; it is the outcome of employee *perceptions* of that situation. Management may be able to control the former, but the latter are shaped also by social and cultural influences only partly and indirectly within management's reach.

There is a further problem. Management does not enjoy complete freedom of choice in deciding what productive technology to use; how to design jobs; work-flow; control mechanisms; the manner in which discretion and decision-making are to be distributed. There is always *some* extent – varying according to industry – to which it can choose, but the choice is always within certain limits. In every industry management is likely to feel that, to pursue its goals successfully, it has to accept the industry's own particular types of constraints. A decision to develop prototype electronic equipment in an environment of ever-changing technology and markets is also a decision to accept technology, work organisation and group structure which need, for success, to be different from those seen as more appropriate to mass-producing rayon yarn – which in turn are different from those likely to be chosen for the continuous refining of oil. Each of these three production systems can exist in a number of variants – probably more numerous than most managements suppose – but each set of variations will differ from the other two. And management is likely to believe that should it attempt to go beyond these limits and constraints it will pay a price in terms of output, costs, profits or whatever other yardstick it works to. In other words, what is being recognised here is that even if certain forms of work organisation and group structure could offer management a potential benefit in terms of employee attitudes and motivation, many managements might be conscious that adoption of these forms would involve costs in excess of the benefits – costs produced by the use of organisation patterns which were uneconomic for the particular job in hand. This is to say no more – and no less – than that the organisation of work according to society's present institutions and values often constrains management into constructing work systems which may subject rank and file to frustration of their social and psychological needs. Although this may seem a statement of the obvious it was denied by the dictum which could so easily be drawn from the Human Relations approach that 'the happy and contented worker is the efficient worker,' and *vice versa*. It was a dictum responsible for many disappointments. It ignored the possibility that the technological conditions which made a worker economically productive might also make him unhappy and discontented. Despite the hopes of a few, the stubborn truth remained that the technological and organisational forms which best served management's ends were not necessarily compatible with the social and psychological fulfilment of the rank and file, and there is hardly need to stress which was likely to receive priority.

ECONOMIC MAN AND HIS SIGNIFICANCE FOR MANAGEMENT

In any case we noted earlier in this chapter the fallacy of assuming that social needs are necessarily high in the practical priorities of employees. The norms and values they generate within their informal groups are often related, not to social needs as the Human Relations approach defined them, but to economic welfare, economic security and freedom from arbitrary rule in their pursuit of these ends. This brings us, then, to further sets of structural influences on employee behaviour. We have just seen how different technological, engineering and related organisational factors can evoke different employee responses with respect to the formation of attitudes, grievances and the manner in which they are expressed and pursued – differences for which Human Relations techniques had only a partial and limited relevance. Now we need to note that employees' economic needs interact with pay systems and pay structures in ways which often create problems that certainly call for management skills, but not those skills described by Human Relations as 'social'.

There is hardly need to emphasise that men doing work from which opportunities for intrinsic satisfaction have been largely excluded are likely to view their jobs principally in terms of the extrinsic rewards of pay and the security attending those rewards. They will not necessarily be discontented with this situation. There is reason to believe that large numbers of wage-earners and lower salary-earners, seeing no practical alternative, come to terms with their presumed destiny by adapting their aspirations accordingly. They expect, or teach themselves to expect, no more from work than the pay packet and perhaps good relationships with a few fellow-workers. Given adequacy along such dimensions, many will declare that they experience 'job satisfaction'. Absence of moral involvement and identification does not necessarily, therefore, mean dissatisfaction for men conditioned not to expect them. It is, however, likely to evoke from them a specially exclusive preoccupation with the cash nexus. Such attitudes are sharpened by the cornucopia of plenty which industrial society displays before them. They are strengthened further by inequalities which we shall examine again later.

Given this central role of pay in the jobs of many wage-earners and lower salary-earners, there is no cause for surprise that managements can be found intensifying the vicious circle by manipulating pay as a direct and immediate incentive to evoke desired behaviour. There is less need for this in high-discretion work. In jobs which have not had the potentiality for high intrinsic involvement designed out, the possibility exists that such a potentiality will generate within the individual a capacity for internal self-discipline which needs neither the stick of close supervision nor the carrot of direct economic incentive. But few rank-and-file jobs retain a significant quota of these potentialities and possibilities, and given that rigorous supervision is diminishingly well-received in industry today, the role of the financial incentive has become even more marked in one form or another. Certainly, with pay as the central feature, men performing such jobs respond to direct financial incentives in a way they rarely do otherwise. Work pace under payment by results tends to be markedly different from work pace under payment by time, though the former system can display off-setting disadvantages which have become increasingly apparent.

Employee responses to payment by results systems have thrown up some of the most familiar examples of group behaviour antipathetic to management interests. Employees may be interested not only in financial rewards but also in the security of those rewards. Fearful that too unrestrained an effort by each to maximise his earnings would result in individual members of the group being found 'surplus to requirements' or in management finding some excuse to cut piece-rates, work-groups have often imposed controls over the effort and earnings of their members, supporting these rules with informal sanctions which expressed group approval or disapproval. The early Human Relations school viewed these efforts not as rational responses to understandable fears but as largely irrational gestures arising from employee frustration and resentment born of management's neglect of their social needs. This view was of a piece with the desire to see the enterprise as needing only the right managerial social and leadership skills to become an integrated structure which provided its members with identity, recognition and a sense of meaning and belonging. To regard what became known as 'restrictive practices' as rational responses to understandable fears, they would have had to take much more seriously the notion that work-groups might reasonably see some of their interests as divergent from management's – not a notion which accorded happily with the Human Relations approach or the social philosophy underlying it.

Neither were Human Relations techniques adequate in themselves to deal with another potent influence on employee behaviour – the dynamics of pay structures. This category of problems was referred to earlier as economic in nature, but this is only partly true. Many of the disputes with which we are familiar are not, in the deepest sense, about money but about justice. A simple example will suffice. If we are told that, on account of our specially valued contribution, we are to receive a salary increase of £350 while colleagues are receiving only £300, our mood is likely to be a cheerful one. If, on the other hand, we discover that while we are to receive £400, they are to receive £450, a certain moroseness would no doubt be evident. What would we be morose about? Clearly not the absolute size of the increase, for we would have been cheerful with less. Our grievance would derive from the *relative* deficiency, which would no doubt cause us to feel a sense of injustice. In other words, differentials in money rewards, rather than the absolute size of the money rewards themselves, are the really explosive issue.

This makes 'fairness' a crucial concept in management/

worker relations. It would present vastly less of a problem were there to be a criterion of fairness on which all could agree. In fact there are many conflicting criteria. To management it may seem only 'fair' that the 'loyal' employee should receive more than the indifferent, the strong and hardworking more than the weak and indolent, or the married more than the unmarried. To employees, who may have learned by experience that such principles can be used to divide and weaken them, these criteria may lack all moral validity. But these are the simplest of divergences, and there are many others. Should we compensate men according to manual skill, responsibility, bad conditions, intrinsically unrewarding work, seniority, organisational profitability, job discretion, training required, cost of living, general principles of reducing inequalities, or any other item in a list which could still be extended? All are advanced as criteria of fairness and all are capable of offering different answers to given problems of differentials.

These problems extend, it is hardly necessary to remind ourselves, far beyond organisational boundaries. Suppose it is thought fair for a constable in rural Dorset to receive the same rate as a constable in Oxford, or for a railway porter in Cornwall to be on a par with a porter in Coventry. This might be defended with the slogan: 'the rate for the job'. Yet the constable in Oxford and the porter in Coventry are poor relations alongside the highly-paid car assembly workers in the same cities. They may feel it unfair that even an unskilled labourer can receive as much as themselves by the mere accident of a job in an industry which is able to pay such high rates simply through the freaks of market and technology. Yet the redress of grievances of this sort would only transfer them to Dorset and Cornwall, for why should porters and policemen be fobbed off with less simply because they live in the country?

Such are the endless dilemmas of money reward. In a society where money can buy so much they are inevitably invested with strong emotions, yet there is widespread failure to grasp their full significance. Economists, government spokesmen, employers and other members of the favoured classes are apt to set store by calculations which show that if all very high incomes were distributed equally it would raise standards per head by only a small margin. They offer such calculations as arguments against egalitarianism. There seems difficulty in grasping that the egalitarian attacks inequality not on grounds of absolute standards but on grounds of moral offensiveness.

Clearly the skills which will serve management best in coping with these complexities are not those required for ministering to employees' needs for identity, recognition and a sense of belonging, but those required for an objective, patient appraisal of the economic aspirations and perceptions of different groups, for an analytical examination of facts and trends in rates and earnings, and for a shrewd judgement of power relations among, and the mood and temper of, the groups under its rule. Lacking access to such skills, management may find the structure of pay and earnings within the organisation so overtaken by anomalies, inequities and contradictions as to become itself a potent source of disorder and disruption among work-groups. Social skills as defined by the Human Relations school will not help management here. That these pay systems and differentials can be an independent structural influence in their own right on employee and group behaviour can be demonstrated by means of an example. We may imagine two plants exactly identical in product, technology, labour force and every other sense except that one is governed by a pay structure which management, by a judicious blend of rational argument, persuasion and power, has preserved as a stable, coherent system largely legitimised by its employees, and the other by a structure which management has allowed to become riddled with what are seen by employees as inconsistencies and anomalies. It is a fairly safe prediction that despite being identical in every other respect the two plants would differ sharply in their record of disputes and distrust.

The same reasoning can be applied to the rest of management's personnel and labour relations policy. If this takes the form, not of a planned and consistent overall strategy, but of piecemeal, hand-to-mouth expedients to meet a succession of emerging problems and issues, the resultant contradictions and confusions can only become another addition to the structural influences which can make management's task of governing more difficult. And, as with the other factors, solutions satisfactory to management are likely to require analytical ability, negotiating flair, insight and courage rather than social skills.

ORGANISATIONAL CHARACTER

Even a manager well-endowed with these qualities and abilities meets a special problem when he takes over what for him is a new command. For he inherits a situation created by predecessors. This proposition may seem as unexceptionable as it is obvious, yet we are apt not to grasp its full significance. Inheriting a situation created by predecessors means inheriting sets of attitudes, assumptions, hopes, fears and expectations among employee groups which others have played a major part in bringing about. One's subordinates, and for that matter one's colleagues and superiors, have a dimension in history which has led them to expect certain things for themselves and to expect certain behaviours from others. These established attitudes and expectations within the organisation play a considerable part in shaping the behaviour of new entrants – including the new manager. The way people perceive and behave towards us is often the major factor in determining how we perceive and behave towards them. If they act with suspicion and distrust it needs a considerable conscious effort on our part not to respond in the same manner.

This tendency illuminates one of the ways in which an organisation may be said to have a character. Applied to management/ worker relations, it means that employee attitudes and expectations brought to bear upon a new manager represent a distillation of their previous experience. In other words, the frame of reference through which they perceive, interpret and evaluate his behaviour and policies will to some extent, however much they aim to 'give the new man a chance', reflect the attitudes and expectations, good or bad, created in them by his predecessors. Unless the newcomer is socially aware to an unusual degree and consciously aspires to break with established patterns of behaviour, he will tend to be drawn by them into certain reciprocatory responses which ensure that the established patterns in fact continue. Thus is the newcomer socialised into the character of the organisation. Social mechanisms of this sort contribute to continuity in organisational processes, a continuity which we all have occasion sometimes to applaud, sometimes to deplore. In some respects we approve the fact that habitual patterns of perceptions and responses ensure the on-going continuance of organisational life, in others we may wish that behaviour were more flexible and quickly adaptable to change. But whatever the balance of our preferences, the tendency of habitual behaviour to persist remains a fact. This is why historical depth is an indispensable dimension of understanding and insight in the field of management/worker relations, as in other types of human interaction.

With this structure of established attitudes and expectations, existing in the form of a diverse set of organisational subcultures, we acknowledge yet another determinant of employee behaviour, the last of which we can take cognizance here. We have been led into this brief review of some of the more important behavioural influences by the need to examine the message which so often seemed to be projected by the Human Relations approach; that the nature of employee behaviour and of relationships with management depended most importantly on management's social skills. Even the limited sketch we have provided for ourselves here indicates that attempts by management to draw employee work-groups into an integrated structure of problem-solving cooperation towards a common purpose are likely to meet with strongly resistant counter-tendencies. Clearly the nature, strength and mode of the employee challenge will vary according to the way in which their aspirations interact with technology, work-flow, control systems, job definitions, pay systems and differentials, company personnel policy and administration, and existing group subcultures.

In practice the situation is even more complex than this, for as we saw from the studies of work-group behaviour the very nature of the aspirations themselves may well be affected by the job situations in which employees find themselves. But what is clear is that many job structures created by the industrial revolution, as perceived by their occupants, generate resistances, grievances and claims which have their roots not in the occupants' need for a sense of belonging and meaningful participation in the organisation, but in the need for furtherance of their economic interests and security and for protection against arbitrary rule and injustice. Indeed, it is precisely the manifest failure of the work organisation as we know it to convince the rank and file that the latter needs will be adequately respected that has so weakened their motivation to behave as willing and cooperative participants. The argument has led us back, in other words, to the proposition that the modern, large-scale work organisation fails, in general, to secure the moral adhesion of its rank and file – which is only another way of saying that it fails to draw them into an integrated community of purpose with top management.

The Human Relations approach, like other strategies we have examined, represents an attempt to retain the economic benefits of hierarchy, extreme division of labour and elaborate authority structures while avoiding their costs as manifested in a largely indifferent or actively hostile rank and file. It seeks, by acting upon employees' supposed social needs, to draw them into an integrated community of purpose without, however, changing the basic structures of job design, reward, decision-making and authority relations within which they are located. The failure of this approach has produced a gradual increase in readiness to look somewhat more searchingly at the nature of the employee's job in its structural context. The attempt to integrate employees purely by means of management styles, personal leadership techniques, and other devices which left work and decision-making structures virtually intact, had not offered the hoped-for return. Perhaps it was time to think whether marginal modifications in such structures could be devised which strengthened employee compliance and motivation but did not involve offsetting losses in technical efficiency. As ideas developed along these lines it became increasingly clear that what was centrally involved here was decision-making and the widely-varying degrees to which members of the organisation participated in it. Our task in the next chapter will be to develop this notion and what it logically implies.

Further Reading

BARITZ, L. *The Servants of Power*. New York: John Wiley and Sons, 1965.

CHILD, J. *British Management Thought*. London: George Allen and Unwin, 1969.

FRIEDMANN, G. *Industrial Society*. Glencoe: The Free Press, 1964.

GOLDTHORPE, J. H., LOCKWOOD, D., BECHHOFER, F., PLATT, J. *The Affluent Worker: Industrial Attitudes and Behaviour*. Cambridge: At the University Press, 1969.

GOLDTHORPE, J. H., LOCKWOOD, D., BECHHOFER, F., PLATT, J. *The Affluent Worker in the Class Structure*. Cambridge: At the University Press, 1969.

ROBINSON, D. (ed.) *Local Labour Markets and Wage Structures*. London: Gower Press, 1970.

SAYLES, L. R. *Behavior of Industrial Work Groups*. New York: John Wiley and Sons, 1958.

SCHEIN, E. H. *Organizational Psychology*. Englewood Cliffs, New Jersey: Prentice-Hall, 1965.

SILVERMAN, D. *The Theory of Organisations*. London: Heinemann, 1970.

TILLETT A., KEMPNER, T., WILLS, G. *Management Thinkers*. Harmondsworth: Penguin Books, 1970.

5. Consent and Participation in Decision-Making

PRESCRIBED AND DISCRETIONARY ASPECTS OF WORK

How can we make sense of the growing emphasis on participation as a central theme in the discussion of employee motivation? The argument will be developed here in terms of participation in decision-making. The first step is to recognise that decision-making is not, as some appear to believe, an activity pursued only at managerial levels. Much discussion seems to assume that decisions are made only by managers. If this is the starting assumption, participation in decision-making by the rank and file comes to seem simply a matter of their participating in other men's decisions – namely those of supervisors and/or the various managerial ranks arrayed above them. This has the consequence of shifting discussion almost at once on to the theme of employee representation on managerial or directorial boards and committees. For although the individual employee may be able to participate directly and personally in certain of the decisions made by his immediate supervisor, the stage is soon reached when his involvement in decisions at higher levels has to be indirect, through representatives. Thus debate tends to revolve round the nature and extent of this indirect, representative participation in which only a tiny proportion of the rank and file are personally involved.

It will be convenient, before exploring the inadequacy of the indirect representation approach, to note the range of managerial decisions which, in theory if not yet in practice, are open to this mode of participation. The discussion can be simplified by means of a crude categorisation which serves to illustrate the possibilities. There are what might be called 'personnel' decisions covering such issues as wage rates and salaries, hours of work, hiring and firing, promotion and transfers, overtime pay, shift arrangements and holidays. 'Social' decisions might be thought to bear on the administration of welfare programmes, health and safety regulations, pension funds and the like. The notion of 'economic' decisions could be used to cover (a) 'technical' issues concerning methods, materials, organisational arrangements, production planning and control, division of labour and the design of jobs, and (b) 'business' issues such as organisational objectives and priorities, markets and sales, expansion or contraction of operations, rationalisation, capital investment, distribution and use of profits, changes in plant organisation, mergers and so on. No significance attaches to the names given to these categories, and the allocation of items to categories is in many cases quite arbitrary. Moreover it is often difficult to treat the categories as separate, for an item in any one may be bound up with items in either or both of the other two. Nevertheless they give some notion of the range over which participation could conceivably extend.

An even wider perspective on participation is afforded, however, once we remember that to see decision-making solely as a managerial activity is fallacious and is bound to distort subsequent discussion. Every job in the organisation, however humble, involves making decisions. Decision-making is simply a process of choosing between alternatives, and no job can be performed without making choices. The chief executive and the board have to decide, for example, the rate and allocation of capital spending; the office cleaner has to decide what degree of thoroughness is appropriate if the job is to be completed before the staff arrive. In making choices between alternatives the employee, at whatever level, is exercising discretion. Without the opportunity to choose between alternatives there can be no decision-making and therefore no discretion. Thus since every job calls for choices, every job may be said to have discretionary content, though there are obvious – and very wide – differences in the amount and importance of the discretion vested in different jobs. Equally obviously, no job consists wholly of discretionary content. Discretion is always exercised within certain prescribed limits, which in a job are those that leave the occupant no discretionary choice, and therefore involve him in no decision-making. The decision has already been made. It comes to him in the form of a prescription and he is required only to obey it. The chief executive and the board make choices within limits set by contractual obligations, collective agreements, company law, insurance stipulations, health and welfare legislation, and a host of other constraints which in effect deprive them of discretion over a wide sector of their behaviour. The office cleaner works within prescribed limits set by arrival and departure times, by the areas of responsibility allocated, and by the implements and materials supplied.

The difference between the prescribed and the discretionary aspects of work can also be presented in terms of specific and diffuse obligations. The prescribed elements impose upon the job occupant certain specific obligations – as when the manager instructs his secretary always to keep in stock a specified number of the appropriate postage stamps to deal with the day's posting of mail. Discretionary elements, on the other hand, impose diffuse obligations. There are no specific definitions laid down and the job occupant has to make a personal judgement as to what is required (in other words, make a decision) – as when the manager instructs his secretary only to be careful to keep 'enough' stamps in stock and leaves it to her discretion how many is enough.

Thus in designing a job, or in other words defining the nature of its duties, the job designer has to decide which aspects of the job to leave to the discretion of the occupant, and which to prescribe for him in the form of choices already made (decisions already taken). Prescriptions can be embodied not only in contractual and legal obligations and negotiated commitments, but also in machinery, jigs and patterns, programmed procedures, budgetary controls, and operating rules of many diverse kinds. From this point of view, the organisation can be seen as a continuing series of decision-making events within prescribed limits, and we can ask of it the all-important question: How are these powers of decision-making distributed throughout the system? Or, to put the same question another way: In what diverse ways and to what diverse degrees do the various members of the organisation participate in this total process of decision-making that constitutes the organisation as an on-going concern?

We are thus now using the currently fashionable language of 'participation in decision-making', but with one important difference. As we have noted, this phrase usually refers to some form or another of participation in other men's decisions, as when supervisors and managers practise so-called 'participative management' by inviting the subordinate to contribute in some way to their decision-making, or when employees serve on consultative or policy-making committees with management, or participate as representatives on directorial boards. The present analysis, however, emphasises that the individual's own job also determines, by the degree of discretion it carries, how far he participates in the total process of decision-making which the organisation requires.

With this in mind we can ask of any employee two crucial questions: first, how many, and what quality of, decisions is he able to make in his own job, and second, what degree of influence does he have upon other men's decisions in which he may feel to have an interest?

DECISION-MAKING AND MORAL INVOLVEMENT

The significance of these questions for the themes explored in this book has been implicit in some of the propositions advanced earlier, but it must now be made explicit. There is growing reason for believing that, in our kind of society, the degree of moral involvement and identification generated within the individual towards his work situation depends primarily on the degree and nature of the discretion it directly and personally affords him. There are, of course, some who are temperamentally averse to this kind of involvement in work, or who have been irreversibly conditioned by family, subculture and their own work experience to expect or demand none. These may opt for low-discretion work and resist any change in it. But observation suggests a widespread capacity among men to develop a moral involvement as their job makes greater and deeper demands on them, and conversely, to become to some degree alienated and indifferent if it requires only mechanical performance of routine activities planned and designed by others. Should this be so there would be no occasion for surprise. The greater the extent to which one's job requires only the performance of tasks already programmed and decided upon

97

by others, to the relative exclusion of choices made by oneself, the less one's individual self is involved in the activity. The old term 'factory hands' can thus be seen to be highly appropriate, for the mind, heart and spirit are not being invited to partici- pate. The faculty most in demand is that of obedience to pre- scribed rules – given, of course, whatever training may be needed. This does not seem the sort of job situation likely to evoke from most people subjected to it a contribution of moral involvement and personal identification. Such a contribution is more likely, for most of us, to be evoked by a situation in which we are called upon to express our individual and unique self through the exercise of choices in a process of decision- making about issues to which we attach significance.

Here we can establish links between the language of discre- tion and of trust relations. This use of the word 'trust' refers not to the personal relationships involved in face-to-face contacts, but to trust – or distrust – insofar as it is embodied in the rules, roles and other policies and arrangements which some men make for others. The greater the degree of discretion extended to a person in his work, the more he feels that the relevant rules and arrangements embody a high degree of trust. This high trust suggests to him that those controlling his work destinies see him as one of their own fraternity, to be treated with respect as an individual person whose interests must be considered. Such a relationship is likely to generate in him something of the personal involvement being discussed here.

Conversely, the occupant of a job of low discretion, hedged about with prescriptive rules, checks, controls, inspection and close supervision, is likely to feel this job definition embodies low trust. This may suggest to him that his masters are exclud- ing him from their own high-trust fraternity – that they see him as no more than an instrumental and inferior means to their purposes, who need not be treated any more favourably than labour market forces demand or than collective pressure with his fellow-employees can exact. Here we move towards the impersonal, contractual, low-trust relationship which yields so little of the moral involvement we are discussing, thereby exem- plifying the specific type of relationship as against the diffuse kind more characteristic of high-discretion work. It must be repeated, however, that the use of 'trust' terminology in this

discussion does not rest on its ordinary sense of personal relationships. Industry has had more than enough of well-meant
admonitions that its participants must be nicer to one another.
It cannot be too strongly emphasised that this is not what is
being suggested here. The proposition is that, quite apart from
personal trust or distrust between particular people, there can
be said to be 'institutionalised' trust or distrust which is embodied in the social arrangements, decisions and policies which
men seek to impose on each other.

It is not, to be sure, inevitably the case that a low-discretion
role has a depersonalising, alienating effect on the occupant.
We noted earlier that a person may willingly apply himself to
the humblest role in a spirit of strong personal commitment
provided he shares the objectives of his leaders. He may not
derive much zest or fulfilment from his actual task activities as
such, but he discharges them conscientiously in the knowledge
that they serve a cause which he supports and respects. We
also observed, however, that such attitudes do not seem common among the rank and file of modern large-scale industry.
Preceding chapters have shown how employers and managers,
increasingly conscious that the great benefits of modern material
and social technology were being partially offset by a shortfall
in rank-and-file commitment of this kind, have tried to induce
in employees a sense of common interests and diffuse, high-trust
relations. Welfare programmes, the philosophy underlying
Taylor's strategy of Scientific Management, the early Human
Relations approach via social integration – these have been
examined as attempts to retain the advantages of large-scale
organisation, extreme division of labour, hierarchy and full
managerial control, while at the same time avoiding their disadvantages. Although not wholly without their benefits for
management, they have generally failed to evoke the spirit
sought by their more hopeful exponents, for the reason – as this
book would argue – that they aspired to generate a high-trust
response from what employees experience as a low-trust situation. The structure and definitions of work roles and of organisational decision-making in general remained essentially
unmodified. All that changed was that management tried to
induce low-discretion employees to perceive the situation in
high-trust terms. For the most part it failed in the face of the

stubborn facts of modern, bureaucratic, industrial organisation.

Events were to show, however, that other shots could yet be found in the managerial locker. A few diverse initiatives began to explore the possibilities inherent in the notion of participation in decision-making. But still the strategy remained one of effecting only minimal changes in the orthodox, managerially-dominated structure. The fear persisted that greater participation by the individual rank-and-file employee in terms of an enlarged discretion in his own job would threaten the economic advantages of division of labour, hierarchy and managerial control. The policy continued, therefore, of trying to secure what was seen as the best of both worlds. Since the tried and tested advantages of bureaucratic organisation were being marginally offset by negative responses from the rank and file, the rigours of hierarchical bureaucracy were to be softened somewhat in the hope of strengthening employee compliance, loyalty and involvement. No significant enlargement was to be made in the employee's participation in terms of decision-making in his own job. But he was to be given a limited influ-ence, often necessarily an indirect one through representatives, upon the decision-making of supervisors, higher managers or perhaps even directors. The theory rested on the assumption (certainly valid for some cultures but not necessarily all) that a degree of participation in decisions affecting them, even if only limited and indirect, disposes men to comply more readily. This limited influence might require management on some occasions to bend from its first preferences, but the calculation was that this danger could be sufficiently contained.

Given, then, that after the Second World War discussion was turning to the possible value to management of a limited and contained employee participation in managerial decision-making, one might suppose that the already deeply-rooted institution of collective bargaining, by which representatives of both sides negotiate decisions about terms and conditions of employment and the settling of employee grievances, would already have been welcomed long ago by employers as a major contribution to the promotion of compliance. And indeed by some it was. Yet it is doubtful if many managers, called upon to direct their thoughts to the subject of participation in managerial decision-making, turn first to collective bargaining. Rather do they tend to think first of participative management, participation in terms of representation on advisory or consultative committees, or a minority voice on directorial boards. What accounts for this selective interest? In suggesting answers to this question we shall find ourselves exploring some of the principal characteristics of these various forms of participation and the responses they evoke from management and employee collectives.

PARTICIPATION THROUGH COLLECTIVE BARGAINING

Participation in decision-making through collective bargaining has become by far the most widespread and important form in Western industrial societies. Although there has always been, and remains, a tradition of resistance to it among some employers and managers, it has come to be seen by many as a valuable and even indispensable mechanism for negotiating and preserving order over the large aggregates of employees and complex occupational structures increasingly characteristic of industrial society. With this growth of organisational scale has come a managerial need for complex patterns of rules and usages governing rewards, work arrangements, hiring, firing, discipline, and the handling of individual and group grievances. These in turn have raised problems of securing employee compliance with rules, their detailed application, and possible alteration.

It is in this context that some managements have come to see the representative procedures of collective negotiation and grievance settlement as having a positive contribution to make in promoting consent among the governed and serving as an instrument of bureaucratic administration. Certainly this has become established as the received view of most governments, relevant agencies and specialist opinion in Western countries.

This does not necessarily imply that managements will see collective bargaining as the only, or even the main, strategy for handling their labour force. From their point of view it may have certain inadequacies or indeed positive disadvantages which partially or wholly offset its usefulness. In the first place, compliance with rules is not the same as high moral involvement in an identification with, and commitment to, one's work situation. Collective bargaining can promote compliance by virtue of being a process through which employees secure, indirectly through representatives, a voice in the making of decisions immediately important to them. Such a process can, given the conditions noted in the first chapter, strengthen the legitimacy of the rules in the eyes of the governed and thus increase the chances of their being accepted and obeyed. It also offers a channel of communication that may be more effective in articulating problems and grievances than the line of managerial authority. There was no reason to suppose, however, that collective bargaining would generate within the individual employee that positive moral involvement in his job which management might be seeking. The fact that someone is participating on his behalf in other men's decision-making does nothing of itself to enrich the importance and quality of the decisions he is currently called upon to make in his own job.

Moreover, for some managements, collective bargaining might seem more than simply inadequate to promote moral involvement; it might appear to them to be positively opposed. After all, the very concept of bargaining implies perceptions of divergent interests. Admittedly there is scope for wide variations in the degree of divergence, conflict and mutual hostility. While this may, at one extreme, be so severe as to threaten organisational survival, it can take a form sufficiently mild as to approximate to the problem-solving type of situation that we examined earlier. But collective bargaining can never be pure problem-solving as management yearns for it, since the trade union or work-group collective can never concede that there exists a total unity of interests between itself and management. There always persists, in the collective's view of events, an element of 'us' and 'them', a perception of 'the two sides'. This is likely to make its participation in decision-making somewhat threatening for management, for here are employees as a collective force taking up an oppositional stance on what may prove an ever-widening range of issues which might end in a fundamental challenge to management's basic prerogatives. Such considerations convince many managements that, useful and necessary though collective bargaining may be, it has to be supplemented by efforts to overcome or minimise its divisive influence. Hence the search for a strategy, to be operated in parallel with collective bargaining, which will, as far as possible, integrate rank and file into a common team effort with the higher levels under management's leadership. Could they be drawn into such an integrated involvement in a way which, besides minimising the threat to managerial power constituted by representative employee participation on a collective bargaining basis, also minimised changes in job design and the distribution of decision-making which might threaten the benefits of division of labour and managerial control? There seemed to be a number of possibilities.

PARTICIPATIVE SUPERVISION

The Human Relations approach had thrown up an idea later developed as participative, consultative or permissive supervision. If, as this approach argued, the uncooperative responses so frequently found among rank-and-file employees were due to management's failure to provide for the expression of their salient need – the need to feel they were making a valued contribution to a group purpose – the answer seemed plain. Management must contrive that this employee need, which was presumed to be all-important for motivation in work, was somehow satisfied. Employee commitment and loyalty would then become focused upon this source of satisfaction. The way would be clear for supervision and higher management to harness the moral involvement thus offered and direct it along pro-management instead of anti-management channels.

But this was easier said than done. How could the employee doing an anonymous fragmented job on extreme division of labour principles be persuaded that his role was a significant and individually meaningful one? The possibility mooted was that his supervisor, suitably trained in Human Relations techniques, might draw him into some degree of consultation and participation in the decisions immediately governing his work life. Perhaps even the small work-group of which he was a member might be so involved as a collective unit. The hopes reposed in such manipulative techniques led to a proliferation of Human Relations courses for supervisors and middle managers.

Why has this approach been given a label so pejorative as 'manipulative'? Why should an attempt to enlarge, however slightly, the individual's insight into, and influence over, his work situation be described in terms carrying an overtone of disparagement? The answer is that the employee was offered this minimal consultation in supervisory decision-making not for what it might contribute to the fulfilment of his own purposes and personality but for what it could contribute to management's objectives. That this was so became apparent as soon as the possibility was envisaged of the employee making an 'unsuitable' or 'inappropriate' contribution or response to supervisory decision-making – i.e., one which ran counter to management's interests. To be sure, he might only rarely have the opportunity to do so even under a Human Relations strategy. In practice its application proved more likely to be confined to explanations of why a particular managerial decision or policy took the form it did. Here and there, however, employees might be allowed to make rather larger choices than previously – for example, to vary the speed of a conveyor belt during the shift. Only if, over a period, they made the 'right' choices and the experiment threw up no incidental problems was it likely to be continued. It was always a safe prediction that 'mistaken' initiatives or inconvenient choices would be at best kindly 'corrected' and at worst simply overridden.

In fact, most of the Human Relations literature tactfully passed over such embarrassing possibilities. The assumption was either that employees could always be brought, by skilful 'leadership', to use their participative opportunities along lines acceptable to management, or that if this seemed unlikely then management would realise the circumstances to be 'inappropriate' for participative supervision. What justifies the description of this approach as manipulative is that it sought to exploit a presumed human need for purposes which were rarely explicitly stated. The literature often spoke of treating employees as ends in themselves, but the underlying assumption was clearly that the whole approach only made sense insofar as it served managerial purposes. For all the talk of a recognition by business of its social and moral responsibilities, rank-and-file employees were no more being treated as ends than in the harshest years of pioneering industrialism. They were still handled instrumentally as means; all that had changed (for a small minority) were views as to the most effective methods of handling. It can hardly be otherwise so long as men are constrained and controlled, in their productive activities, to work to ends and means which they have no effective voice in defining, whether the ultimate end is private profit or 'the public interest' as determined by a government.

In the event, participative supervision was to prove no Holy Grail. Some of the reasons are identical with those advanced in the last chapter to explain the more general weaknesses of the Human Relations approach. But there are others. Employees conditioned to expect and accept authoritarian rule were as likely to be bewildered as gratified if the style suddenly changed. Bewilderment was likely to pass into suspicion when it became clear that the new style was not an open-ended invitation for employees to participate in ways which might conceivably lead anywhere, but a technique by which management sought to pursue its ends more effectively while at the same time convincing the managed that they were being given a significantly greater voice in their work experience. With respect to this as to many other techniques of personnel policy, management showed a greater capacity to deceive itself than to deceive employees. Some managers, no doubt, convinced themselves that they were introducing a new concept of treating men as significant ends in their own right. Perhaps they felt that a genuine ethical development was being frustrated when their superiors indicated, as many did, that disappointing results, the return of bad times, or the danger of the new style getting inconveniently out of hand, rendered desirable the resumption of more conventional patterns. We need to recall what we have noted elsewhere, that individual managers may well be allowed, indeed encouraged, by their seniors to pursue, and to speak with full ethical conviction about, policies which for them have a genuine moral content – provided these are viewed by seniors as compatible with 'organisational interests'. Those with the ultimate power of decision are likely to have no objection to subordinate managers harbouring moral convictions about how employees should be treated – so long as these convictions appear to serve what they define as organisational well-being.

PARTICIPATION THROUGH JOINT CONSULTATION

Participative supervision caught on more in America than in Britain, partly because the hope of stemming union influence by means of integrative personnel policies had remained more widespread and vigorous there. But this is only a matter of degree: Britain, too, witnesses managerial practices which seek to strengthen the integration of the lower ranks into managerial purposes and values. One which received special emphasis for some years after the Second World War was joint consultation. Government and progressive management circles hoped that employee consent could be strengthened and motivation quickened through the voluntary adoption of formally constituted committees, representative of management and employees, which met regularly and discussed common interests in a problem-solving manner. Whereas bargaining focused on the issues that divided the parties, joint consultation was to promote constructive cooperation on the issues presumed to unite them – such as those matters relevant to the economic success of the organisation and its ability to supply all members with a rising standard of living. This share in the managerial process beyond the range normally covered by collective bargaining would, it was hoped, release the potential for creative involvement which resided within the rank and file. Existing job structures and organisational design would not be affected, and managerial retention of control seemed ultimately assured by the fact that the committees were no more than advisory bodies through which management 'collected the voices', ideally before rather than after making its decisions. In these respects the movement was an expression of the Human Relations belief that the postulated rank-and-file need for cooperative involvement could be met – and managerial benefits derived thereby – without conceding any real change in the power structure and organisational design of the enterprise.

Joint consultation proved no more a panacea, however, than all the preceding and succeeding devices about which such great hopes have been entertained by a minority of enthusiasts. Here and there a company might count modest gains – joint consultation could sometimes be fruitful where it constituted a further expression of an existing relationship of confidence between the parties. But as a universal key for releasing the cooperative potential of the rank and file it passed through the usual stages of being greeted with fashionable enthusiasm and then declining to the role of just another technique which companies might or might not find marginally worth having, depending on history, personalities and circumstance.

The reasons for disappointment can be deduced from the preceding analysis. Whatever the joint consultation process might do for those few who as representatives actually took part, there seemed no reason to suppose it would transform the perceptions and motivations of their constituents, whose jobs and subjection to hierarchical authority and control remained unchanged. Once again, it expressed the eternal managerial hope that men could be induced to offer high-trust, problem-solving behaviour in a situation whose structural features they had come to see in low-trust terms.

If joint consultation offered little to the wage-earner on the shop floor or the clerical worker in his office, there was not much of enduring value either for the trade union officer or shop steward. At worst it might seem a device by which management hoped to undermine rank-and-file loyalty to their collective organisations and thereby weaken them. At best it was only really valuable to the extent that management could be induced to commit itself to a mutually-agreed policy on issues important to the unions and their members. But the further the situation moved in this direction the more it had to be seen as a bargaining relationship rather than an advisory and consultative one. Admittedly there might be matters in which employee representatives had an interest but on which they lacked the strength to press management into making a binding commitment. Here it could be useful for them to have an extra channel of communication through which to urge upon management certain views and opinions. But as shop-floor representatives gained confidence and strength they pressed not simply for management's ear but for its readiness to enter into binding commitments on the issues important to them. As against merely 'making representations', which management might choose to ignore, or helping management to solve its problems, which might guarantee employees no enhanced share in any favourable outcome, the union or work-group might want management to *commit* itself on certain wider issues of policy just as it did on such conventional bargaining matters as wages and working hours. Given such rising aspirations there was little value for them in what they were increasingly likely to see as a talking-shop from which management emerged committed to nothing.

Management was saying, in effect: 'Contribute your constructive proposals; offer your opinions; advance your judgements – and then trust us to fashion the best policies in the interests of the company and all its members.' But this was precisely what the rank and file, with their structurally induced sense of being used as means to serve their masters' purposes, felt unable to do. As instruments towards other men's ends, they felt the need for specific, defined protections and returns. In this way they expressed the low-trust responses which their job situation engendered in them. From management's point of view, however, the forging of specific commitments converted what it had hoped would be a problem-solving activity into a win-lose bargaining process.* Where management persisted in opposing this trend the employee representatives could well lose interest and allow the consultation machinery to become moribund. Where it accepted the trend the distinction between consultation and bargaining lost whatever practical reality it may have had and logic pointed to the abandonment of separate consultative forms.

A similar analytical approach can be turned upon other techniques that have emerged over the years. The belief persists, for example, that to give employees an ownership stake in the enterprise or a share in profits will arouse the desired spirit of involvement, identification and commitment. This is to offer increased participation, not in decision-making, but in the out-

---

* It will be recalled that a problem-solving approach works to an assumption of shared ends and concentrates on clarifying the facts, searching for the best methods, and elucidating the probable consequences of alternatives. The parties do not seek to trap, bluff or score off each other, and do not conceal, distort or manipulate information and ideas. These are characteristics of a high-trust situation. In bargaining relationships the parties are conscious of divergent ends and therefore bring pressure to bear on each other, using gamesmanship, bluff and concealment or manipulation of information and ideas. These are characteristics of a low-trust situation.

come of the organisational effort. There is no evidence, however, of any lasting effect upon the employee whose job remains fragmented, highly prescribed, and subject to hierarchical inspection, supervision and control. The destinies of the enterprise are moulded, as he well knows, by events and decisions, both within and without the organisation, which lie far above and beyond any conceivable control or influence of his. His role is simply not strategically important enough in discretionary terms for him to feel that any extra commitment from him will have significant effects on the total outcome. His effort becomes swallowed up in the complex aggregate of other men's efforts, many of them vastly more influential than his own.

PARTICIPATION THROUGH EMPLOYEE-DIRECTORS

More recently Britain has witnessed a quickening interest in the idea of employee-directors on company boards. This is being fed by assumptions derived from envious glances at West Germany and other European countries. Entry into the European Economic Community has enlarged somewhat the awareness that West Germany, for example, makes legal provision for labour representation on company supervisory boards which oversee the management boards responsible for day-to-day business, and in certain industries for labour representation on the management boards themselves. This knowledge contributes to a certain picture of labour relations in West Germany, a picture with some basis in fact but losing nothing in journalistic heightening and adornment. It is a picture of total management/worker harmony, keenly motivated workers offering willing cooperation in order to maximise economic growth, and a happy absence of opposition-minded shop steward organisation on the shop floor. We cannot attempt here to assess the validity of this view. The crucial point is that, with the usual tendency to draw over-hasty conclusions about cause and effect, the assumption is being made that the allegedly halcyon state of labour relations in West Germany is a direct and simple consequence of the arrangements for labour participation in managerial decision-making. This is contributing to interest in the idea of employee-directors as found on regional boards of the nationalised British Steel Corporation, a subject explored by Brannen (forthcoming).

Both top management and employee collectives might feel they had something to gain from this innovation. However vigilant managers try to be in keeping their ears to the ground, differences of status and authority often prevent their getting a full picture of feeling and opinion among rank and file. Employee-directors could be expected to make a contribution in this respect. Moreover, they could supply an extra dimension to management's appreciation of rank-and-file attitudes and behaviour – a sympathetic understanding of the *reasons* for those attitudes and behaviour – not a dimension along which management is usually well endowed, and one which could be crucial in shaping a successful personnel and labour relations policy. Information and insight of the right quality could enable management to gauge better the probable consequences of alternative policies and to formulate more appropriate strategies of response to the expected outcomes.

For their part, the unions and work-group collectives might also enjoy gains. Given the appropriate relationship with the employee-directors – a crucial condition – they would have a voice in deliberations about policy. True, it would be no more than a voice, and a small minority voice at that. But they could use it both to seek information and to offer reasoned statements in support of preferred policies, though admittedly the managerial directors could choose to be niggardly with the first and dismissive of the second. As with conventional joint consultation, this is not a process through which either side enters into a commitment with the other. A meeting of a directorial board or committee of management is not a process by which management seeks to secure employee acceptance of, and commitment to, certain agreed policies and decisions, or *vice versa*; it is a problem-solving and programme-determining process by which management fixes the policies and decisions it wants to apply. Employees are aware that 'their' directors are not in a negotiation situation, constitute one voice among many, and have no power to press their interests and views with any force, but they may nevertheless think it useful to have this voice.

Conversely, they may come to feel that the direction of influence is too often in the wrong direction – that their men are succumbing to the argument and persuasion of top management. The union or work-group may in any case come to want far more than is yielded by the appointment of representatives to policy-making and problem-solving procedures. As emerged in our discussion of joint consultation, the collective may want management to *commit* itself on certain wider issues of policy. It may aspire to nominate the employee-directors, treat them as mandated delegates, brief them on their contribution to policy discussions, and provide formal procedures for reporting back. The more rigorously the collective pursues this approach the greater the likelihood of the directorial board meeting becoming a negotiating arena in which the employee-directors press predetermined views and try to induce the managerial directors to commit themselves.

If management insists that these wider issues be dealt with only within the problem-solving, policy-making context, it is by the same token refusing to negotiate on them. It would not be surprising, therefore, if employee collectives were to show only limited enthusiasm for an employee-director arrangement of this kind. The situation is one in which management does not negotiate, but simply collects the voices and subsequently makes its own decision – the employee-directors being, of course, in a minority, though clearly at risk of being identified, or at least associated, with policies and decisions which prove unpopular. There is a possibility that the collective will appear to share responsibility for certain decisions without having been able to exert upon the making of these decisions even such power as it can normally deploy in the bargaining situation.

Should the collective succeed in escaping from this position of responsibility without power by inducing top management to 'negotiate' on the wider issues concerned (in the sense of committing itself to policies agreed with employee directors acting as mandated union spokesmen), then the situation is best described, not as one of employee representatives participating in managerial problem-solving and policy-making, but as one of representatives of both sides participating in the negotiation of joint understandings and agreements. The managerial problem-solving and policy-making will then be carried out elsewhere. To the extent that the directorial meeting becomes a win-lose situation of the power-bargaining kind it cannot be used by the managerial directors for the sort of problem-solving discussion required in the preparation of their own preferred courses of action. Such preparation calls for frank exchanges among themselves on the merits of union or work-group proposals; on the alternative strategies of response; on possible counter-arguments involving the selective use of information; on the tactics and costs of resistance and the psychology of specific concessions and their timing.

Forced into a power-bargaining situation, the managerial directors would no more conduct such discussions in the presence of their employee 'colleagues' than employee collectives would design their policy proposals and negotiating strategy in the presence of top management. Confronted with representatives who adopted an oppositional, win-lose, divergent-interests stance, the managerial directors would feel the need to withdraw their own problem-solving, common-interest discussions to another venue from which the employee directors would be excluded. Nothing, after all, can prevent a group meeting informally in a private house, a club, or even someone's office. Thus if collectives sought to push employee-directors into a power-bargaining situation they would lose access to an additional channel of communication which could conceivably be freer and wider-ranging than that normally prevalent within the negotiation arena. Of course, if collectives felt strong enough to engage in power-bargaining on all the issues about which they sought to press opinions on management this would not matter to them. But just so long as they consider it worth their while to press opinions on certain issues while not wanting or feeling able to challenge management to a power contest about them, they may come to see the employee-director principle as having a certain limited usefulness.

Both sides therefore have to accept the consequences of their choices. Wherever unions or work-groups seek to use such power as they can mobilise to press management into binding commitments, management is likely to reciprocate with the tactics characteristic of power-bargaining, such as bluff, gamesmanship and the selective use of information. On the other hand, a negotiated agreement or understanding means that both sides are committed to specified courses of action or patterns of behaviour. Conversely, a consultative and advisory type of relationship which eschews the pressures and tactical manœuvres of power-bargaining makes possible a freer and wider exchange but binds neither of the parties. For management, of course, this has implications for the securing of consent. It may count as a gain the fact that on a given issue it has not committed itself to a union-influenced pattern of action. The price it pays for this is that it has not secured commitment and consent. Management has to decide for itself the balance of advantages of these various strategies.

With respect to another major theme of this book – the managerial struggle not only to secure consent but also to generate positive moral involvement – neither employee-directors playing the power-bargaining game nor employee-directors confining themselves to consultative problem-solving discussion could be expected to make any contribution. Bargaining is of great consequence to employees, but while it can help management by promoting consent it is unlikely to inspire the individual in the discharge of his own task activities. As for employee representatives who simply participate in high-level policy discussion, these are likely to be viewed with indifference by most of the rank and file. Such procedures may well offer prospects of advancement for the employees personally participating, but this is hardly likely to commend them to those left behind. We are back to the proposition that rank-and-file employees whose low-discretion work allows them only minimal participation at the level of their own job are unlikely to be able to generate much interest in high-level management decisions except insofar as they see these as having a significant bearing upon their own welfare. And towards managerial decisions affecting their own welfare, low-discretion employees are likely, as we have seen, to offer attitudes not of cooperative joint problem-solving but of wary and suspicious bargaining. Should their representatives choose to involve themselves in a problem-solving manner with wider issues, the representatives *themselves* may enjoy a heightened sense of involvement, but there is no reason to assume that this will communicate itself to their constituents, whose attitudes and behaviour are likely to be shaped by their own work experience, which remains unchanged. The possibilities of divergence between representatives and constituents under this kind of arrangement are apparent.

A belief that representatives are likely to bring a bargaining rather than a problem-solving approach to joint deliberations prompts many managements to seek to minimise rank-and-file participation in higher decision-making, more especially if it is controlled by union or work-group. To this end, attempts have often been made to define some levels of decision-making or some types of decision as uniquely managerial in the sense that they must remain permanently entrenched within the prerogative of those officially designated managers for these purposes. There is hardly need to stress that legalistic arguments of this kind have rarely settled the issue and are even less likely to carry weight among employees and unions in the future. There is no arbitrary cut-off point at which employee concern can logically be denied. Potentially this concern extends, as we shall see later, far beyond the organisation itself. Government policy and broad social values and assumptions, for example, shape top management strategies on, say, capital investment, the division of labour and the distribution of rewards, and those affect jobs, incomes, security of employment and other ways in which labour is treated.

PARTICIPATION THROUGH ENRICHED JOB DISCRETION

The discussion so far has revealed the diversity of meanings, aspirations and purposes covered by the term participation. It can refer to a style of supervision or management which seeks to foster a sense in the subordinate of being consulted, but which is often little more than a manipulative exercise designed to mask the authority relationship. It can describe the activities of group or departmental employee representatives on somewhat remote and infrequent committees whose role is limited to receiving the decisions of higher authority *after* they have been made. Both the first (or direct) and the second (or indirect) forms are subject to significant variations. The subordinate may be allowed a degree of genuine freedom of decision by his superiors, who may or may not find this innovation useful and allow it to continue. Representatives on committees may be allowed to press views and preferences upon higher authority *before* final decisions are made. Within collective bargaining procedures, the participation of employee representatives results in higher authority binding itself, after negotiation, to certain agreed courses of action. We shall be taking note later of aspirations categorised under 'workers' control' or 'workers' self-management'. It is not difficult to appreciate that, given these and other variations which can be found, the notion of participation is but the crudest of blanket terms. Confusion is compounded by its application to systems of profit-sharing or co-ownership.

It was also argued earlier in this chapter that any view of participation in decision-making which excludes consideration of how far the subordinate's own job and task activities involve his participation in the total decision-making of the organisation is quite inadequate. As we have noted, there are grounds for believing, in fact, that in our society the individual's degree of moral commitment, identification and involvement is associated with the degree of discretion his job affords him. Compared with this, the significance of such forms of participation as direct influence on the decisions of immediate superiors, or indirect influence, through representatives, on the decisions of more distant authority, seems relatively marginal so far as moral involvement in his own job is concerned, however important they may (or may not) be in promoting compliance with the rules and support for the system in general.

Recent years have seen growing interest in an approach to motivation which does concern itself with the nature of the individual's job. This approach has received widespread discussion and a limited degree of practical application under the name of job enrichment. To enrich a job in this context is to vest it with wider and more significant responsibilities – to change it in ways which can be summed up as an enlargement and enrichment of discretion. By the same token, such changes enlarge and enrich the individual's participation in the decision-making of the organisation. The expectation is that, given a keener consciousness of his personal involvement as a consequence of this enlarged role, the employee responds with a stronger commitment.

Such changes in job definitions – and the changes in supervisory relationships and organisational arrangements often consequential upon them – have sometimes been introduced by management fiat and sometimes by negotiation with unions and work-groups. On occasions they have been combined with reforming pay structure, overtime arrangements and work allocation in a comprehensive exercise of productivity bargaining. Examples now to hand reveal a variety of possibilities. In some cases, mass-production, conveyor-belt jobs, previously fragmented down in approved Scientific Management style to highly-prescribed, minimum-discretion functions each performed by a separate specialist operator, have been enlarged in a way which enables each operator to combine a number of functions. The hope inspiring such changes may be no more than to relieve monotony and reduce labour turnover and absence. The enlargement of discretion they introduce may well be small – indeed insignificant. More noteworthy changes have been those in which, for example, production workers are trained to carry out maintenance and minor repair tasks, or in which craftsmen are given increased freedom to schedule their own work. Most significant of all, perhaps, are changes which go beyond the individual to his immediate work-group. Some experiments have vested control over certain decisions within the small work-group under its own leader. The notion of the 'responsible, autonomous group' will possibly prove one of the more important growth points in this field.

JOB ENRICHMENT: SOME CAVEATS

Like so many preceding strategies, job enrichment is being oversold. Its more enthusiastic exponents present it as a panacea of universal application, and against this a number of *caveats* must be entered. One of them concerns the attitudes, values and aspirations of those to whom the strategy is applied. Here there is need to enlarge on a qualification we have already applied to one of the major propositions referred to in this book. Reference has been made to the association between the degree of involvement felt by the individual in his job and the degree of discretion with which it endows him. But we have also seen that in explaining these attitudes of involvement we must not rest content with an objective description of the rules, tasks and discretionary content of the work role itself. Equally important is how the job occupant perceives and responds to them. We can imagine some persons who, placed in a high-discretion role, would respond not with moral involvement and identification but with psychological discomfort, unease and insecurity. Feelings of incompetence might be one cause. Another might be the fact of being temperamentally the sort of person who is happiest within a highly structured, clear-cut and programmed situation and who dislikes the uncertainties, ambiguities and general diffuseness of high-discretion situations which require him to make important choices and accept the consequences. But a third, and a very significant one for our purposes, might be that the individual in question had already adapted himself – having been encouraged to do so by family, friends, school and early work experience – to the assumptions that work could not be expected to yield any significant intrinsic satisfactions, must be undertaken largely for its pay packet, and cannot play a central role in his interests and self-development.

This is specially important in that there are grounds for believing that considerable numbers of those growing up in wage-earning families and wage-earning social environments are in fact conditioned to take just such attitudes as these towards work. They are not necessarily irreversible. Men who have not hitherto taken work seriously as a possible source of intrinsic satisfaction may nevertheless be open to such an orientation if opportunity offers, and even if they begin by resisting – or at least being nervous of – enlarged discretion and responsibility, may learn by experience of their enriched job that they value the change for reasons additional to any increase in monetary reward it may offer. They might, as a result of increased personal involvement, feel somewhat more at one with management in certain respects. They may, if the increase in discretion is significant enough, become rather more conscious of being trusted, of being a member of a team. Such responses could well take behavioural forms which management would find valuable.

But quite different responses are possible. Some individuals and groups may be so powerfully conditioned to see work purely in terms of the pay packet that for all practical purposes their attitudes are irreversible, no matter what alternative type of work experience they are offered. Another possibility is that they have become so habituated to take a wary, low-trust stance towards management's purposes and values that they cannot be weaned away by changes in work roles towards a closer identification with their job and the organisation.

These considerations remind us that in the ordinary course of events men take up higher-discretion jobs with appropriately matching attitudes and aspirations. The individual singled out for promotion is likely to be ready, indeed eager, for greater responsibilities and to have suggested by his behaviour that he is able to offer an increasing involvement and identification with the organisation. The technician, scientist, engineer, manager or academic is likely to have been socialised by family, school or university into a conception of himself as pursuing a career which must yield not only the desired material and status rewards but also work which is intrinsically satisfying and meaningful. In industry as we have hitherto known it, therefore, the likelihood of men faced with high-discretion jobs bringing to their task a totally incongruent set of aspirations and values is relatively small. And given that they are motivated to accept and apply themselves to their high-discretion roles, these roles are likely to evoke from them the appropriate attitudes. Hence the confidence with which reference has been made in earlier arguments to the association between high-discretion work and moral involvement.

In the case of job enrichment, however, management is offering enlarged discretion to those who do not necessarily bring to that offer a congruent set of attitudes and values. Their responses in terms of behaviour will not necessarily, therefore, take those forms of involvement and identification for which management hopes. There is no reason, however, to suppose that such managerial ventures are destined for universal disappointment or anything like it. Certainly one would expect them to encounter setbacks. Individuals so set in their ways that they dread any variation; groups which see the proposed changes as disrupting, say, long-standing social relationships which they greatly value; groups with an anti-management stance so strongly nourished by tradition and experience that it proves resistant to all managerial wooing – these are obvious possibilities. But equally there are signs of a readiness among many lower-level employees to accept an enlarged discretion in their work and to apply themselves within it in ways that meet management approval.

More important limits to job enrichment are set by economic considerations relating to the division of labour. However lyrically some enthusiasts present it as a new dawn in which management is at last treating its employees not as mere means but as ends in themselves, job enrichment is no more than the latest in the long series of management attempts to integrate the rank and file into its own values and purposes. This being so, it will be viewed by management in terms of the benefits and costs it appears to offer, however diffuse, long-term and difficult of quantification these benefits and costs may seem. To the extent that the existing division of labour is seen as producing significant costs in terms of turnover, absence, wastage, indifferent work and other symptoms which express alienation and lack of employee involvement, management may aspire to reduce these costs by modifying the division of labour in the direction of greater discretion at rank-and-file level. Clearly there is nothing inevitable about it so aspiring, even assuming its awareness of these costs, for it may calculate that the economic benefits of the present division of labour are such that even marginal changes would result in losses which outweighed any gains derived from greater employee involvement. Such a line of thought suggests that job enrichment will be pursued up to, but not beyond, the point at which its presumed benefits threaten to be offset by losses produced by the movement away from the extreme division of labour.

To say this is certainly not to assume that a movement away from extreme division of labour *necessarily* involves costs. A change in material technology, for example, may require for its most efficient operation a change in social technology in the direction of greater discretion for rank-and-file operatives. In this way management may enjoy an unplanned and unexpected benefit in terms of employee involvement purely as a consequence of technological change. Some applications of automation and other forms of advanced technology have demonstrated such an effect. This has led to optimistic projections that as advanced technology takes over we shall witness a widespread enlargement of rank-and-file discretion in work, and with it their closer integration with management values and purposes.

I

This line of argument can be disputed on two grounds. First, it probably overestimates the applicability of automation and advanced technology generally, and underestimates the extent to which mass-production concepts, extreme division of labour and the Scientific Management approach will still seem to offer substantial economic returns in major sectors of manufacturing industry. Second, the argument exaggerates the effect on employee attitudes of job enrichment as it has been practised so far. Even in technologically favourable conditions, job enrichment has not, so far as present evidence appears to carry us, resulted in jobs that are seriously comparable, in respect of discretion, with those of middle and upper managers, engineers, scientists, lawyers and others of similar high-discretion status. As a consequence, it has not generated among those affected a comparable set of attitudes and values. Even job-enriched groups which demonstrate more positive and favourable attitudes towards their work and towards management show no disposition to dismantle their defences and integrate with management by abandoning trade unionism and collective bargaining.

This suggests that they see the essential features of their relationship with top management as remaining unchanged, in that they are hired to serve the pursuit of purposes and policies from whose determination and control they are excluded. Still treated as inferior by every consideration of financial reward, status and respect, they have no reason to abandon their consciousness of being viewed by management in low-trust terms so far as work roles, authority structures and control systems are concerned. They therefore continue to return low-trust responses in the sense of withholding full integration and maintaining independent protective organisations based on an assertion of divergent interests. There is no evidence of job enrichment, as at present conceived and applied, overcoming this most palpable and significant evidence of management's failure to integrate the rank-and-file labour force into a fully cooperative unity with managerial, administrative and specialist groups.

Further Reading

BLUMBERG, P. *Industrial Democracy: The Sociology of Participation*. London: Constable, 1968.

BRANNEN, P. *Worker Directors*. London: Hutchinson (forthcoming).

CLEGG, H. A. *A New Approach to Industrial Democracy*. Oxford: Blackwell, 1960.

DANIEL, W. W., MCINTOSH, N. *The Right to Manage*. London: Macdonald–PEP, 1972.

DAVIS, L. E., TAYLOR, J. C. (eds) *Design of Jobs*. Harmondsworth: Penguin Books, 1972

EMERY, F. E., THORSRUD, E. *Form and Content in Industrial Democracy*. London: Tavistock, 1969

FRIEDMANN, G. *The Anatomy of Work*. London: Heinemann, 1961.

HERZBERG, F. *Work and the Nature of Man*. London: Staples, 1968.

JAQUES, E. *Equitable Payment*. Harmondsworth: Penguin Books, 1967.

LIKERT, R. *New Patterns of Management*. New York: McGraw-Hill, 1961.

RHENMAN, E. *Industrial Democracy and Industrial Management*. London: Tavistock, 1968.

STRAUSS, G. 'Some Notes on Power-Equalization' in *The Social Science of Organizations* (ed. H. J. Leavitt). Englewood Cliffs, N.J.: Prentice-Hall, 1963.

STRAUSS, G. 'Workers Participation: A Critical View' in *The Modern Business Enterprise* (ed. M. Gilbert). Harmondsworth: Penguin Books, 1972.

VROOM, V. H., DECI, E. L. (eds) *Management and Motivation*. Harmondsworth: Penguin Books, 1970.

6. Collective Bargaining: Its Role and Meaning

In the preceding chapter an important distinction emerged between those forms of representative participation in managerial decision-making which are designed as problem-solving activities directed towards the pursuit of shared goals, and those which are acknowledged to be bargaining activities deriving from divergent goals. While the facts of industrial life usually bend management (in varying degrees according to industry and country) towards acceptance of the latter, it often remains haunted by a beckoning vision of the former.

The reasons why this vision tends to be so elusive in the circumstances of modern large-scale industry in the West have already been explored. These same reasons have rendered collective bargaining by far the most extensive, significant and deep-rooted form of representative participation in our kind of society. Having noted it earlier on a number of occasions in order to register certain contrasts and support certain arguments, we now need to examine it more closely both in its organisational and (in the next chapter) its wider social context.

As we do so we move towards a tradition of thought and aspiration with respect to workers' participation in decision-making very different from that of participative supervision, joint consultation and minority representation on directorial boards, and indeed extending far beyond collective bargaining itself. The debate about participation ranges much wider than the diverse forms we have already noted. The word has come, in fact, to refer loosely to a whole field of discussion which includes organisational forms more concerned with employee control and self-management than with participation in the limited, managerially-approved forms observable in our own society. We can do no more here, however, than sketch in the more important of these other forms and include, in the book list, suggestions for further reading.

What marks off these forms (and in this respect we must set collective bargaining alongside them) from such devices as participative supervision, joint consultation and employee-directors is that they vest the employee collective (union or organised work-group) with some degree of control over decisions and with some responsibility for them. As we shall see, the possibilities are various. An examination of their relative merits and demerits cannot be undertaken here, for no discussion of how men ought to perceive their rights, duties, privileges and obligations in the context of particular decision-making arrangements can carry weight unless related to the prevailing structure and distribution of rights, duties, privileges and obligations in the wider society outside, and space limitations render discussion on this scale impossible. All that can be said is that decision-making arrangements which might appear to facilitate sectional, self-regarding behaviour by the employee collective (to the detriment, say, of consumer interests, or the technological or commercial viability of the organisation, or government counter-inflationary policy) might properly be criticised in the context, for example, of a society dedicated to the pursuit of equality, but might be argued to be less open to criticism in a society structured so as to make sectional (or individual) self-regarding behaviour the principal mainspring of a highly unequal competitive and acquisitive society.

Against the background of these considerations we return to the various alternatives of participatory control, enumerating them after the manner of Blumberg (1968):

1 Employee representatives may have the right to veto managerial decisions:
   (a) temporarily, after which management either: (i) remains free to implement its decision or (ii) must negotiate with employees (the arrangement sought by engineering unions in Britain);
   (b) permanently (as in the system operated by the Glacier Metal Company).

2 Employees may have the unilateral right of decision (claimed by some forms of craft-type control, workers' 'self-

management' and the like. This system is also receiving a certain limited expression in the shape of the 'autonomous work-group', which is proving a favoured form in the discussion of job enrichment. The 'autonomy' granted by management is of course exercised only within a containing framework of managerial control, and depends for continuance upon its serving managerial purposes.)

3 Employees may have the right of co-decision with management.

At this point we turn from our abbreviated itemisation of alternative forms of control and focus on the commonest form of co-decision, which is, of course, collective bargaining. Its commonest context relates to 'personnel' decisions as categorised earlier, though as far as the employee collective is concerned any type of managerial decision is potentially appropriate for negotiation. The sorts of questions which the collective might well need to ask itself with respect to a particular area of decision-making include the following: Is this of sufficient concern for the union or work-group that we want to induce management to commit itself to an agreed policy about it? Since an agreement implies a commitment on our side, too, what are we likely to have to commit ourselves to? Can we, and do we want to, carry the members with us on that commitment? What processes of communication and consultation are necessary if we are to carry the members with us – in other words if they are to legitimise the commitment?

The last question is crucial, for union and work-group leaders as well as management have problems of winning consent. If, at all levels above the individual's own job, participation in decision-making usually has to be through representatives, problems at once emerge of constructing and maintaining communications between representatives and constituents. Should adequate relationships not be maintained the possibility exists of agreements being reached with management which constituents feel unwilling to honour. The issue is worth examining further, since representative participation in decision-making in some form or another seems likely to increase and may well extend into fields hitherto unfamiliar, and because the question of constituents honouring the consequent agreement or under-standing is widely felt to be of some moment.

One way into the problem is to ask how far management and employee negotiators can regard constituents to be morally, as opposed to merely formally, bound by an agreement in circum-stances where, for example, it transpires that the employee representative failed to acquaint constituents with the relevant issues, choices and information, or has committed them on some issue about which they showed no interest at the time but which later proves to affect them adversely. The distinction between being formally bound and feeling morally bound is crucial; if the former is not supported by the latter the weakness is appa-rent. We need to think harder than hitherto about what proce-dures are going to be regarded as imposing moral obligations on people when representatives conclude agreements on their behalf. In other words, under what conditions and procedures of participation are we going to define constituents as morally bound? The extreme case exemplifies the problem. If an employee representative, be he union officer, shop steward or whatever, takes part in making a decision on an issue without consulting his constituents and without canvassing their opi-nions in any way, it may prove hollow for union and manage-ment if they subsequently insist that 'an agreement has been signed' and that constituents are bound by its terms. If the constituents feel no moral commitment to the agreement and have the power to resist it the possibilities are obvious. Manage-ment and employee representatives have to work out, for their own situation, what are to be the conditions under which con-stituents *will be deemed* to have bound themselves morally to an agreement, and these must include a pattern of systematic communications between representative and constituent.

We noted in Chapter One certain deeper problems concern-ing employee obligation and the honouring of agreements. It was suggested there that in some industrial situations today employee behaviour can only be satisfactorily explained by inferring that they feel little or no sense of moral obligation (as against a sense of expediency) towards the observance of agree-ments. If men subjected to subordination and extreme division of labour in large organisations consider that, despite trade unions and collective bargaining, they remain under a severe power disadvantage *vis-à-vis* management, their awareness of this managerial domination of the system may preclude their feeling any moral attachment to it. For the most part trade unions have sought to strengthen membership observance by stressing the claims of honour. Yet even when members have appeared to accept the implied pluralist assumptions, leaders have often paid too little attention to the conditions which must exist if they are successfully to demand and expect their members' moral adhesion to the agreements concluded on their behalf.

Perhaps the problems of ensuring this moral adhesion are the more acute (a) the higher the level of decision-making at which representative participation takes place, and/or (b) the greater the extent to which the decisions lie within the 'technical' or 'business' categories without having any *immediately apparent* significance for the 'personnel' or 'social' categories. The danger is that because employees evince no present interest in certain issues, representatives may agree to managerial measures which, when their full practical implications emerge, prove unpopular. It is these problems of communication and legitimation which require union or employee representatives to be wary about what they commit themselves to, rather than the usual argument of 'Unions-mustn't-get-involved-in-management-because-they-can't-face-both-ways.'

COLLECTIVE BARGAINING AND MANAGEMENT

That collective bargaining is not a formula for perpetual warfare is well attested by the experience of most Western industrial countries, where compromise agreements negotiated through collective bargaining, usually without disruption, have become the standard pattern governing some of the most central relationships between employer and employed. But although the institution of collective bargaining, far from generating destructive conflict, has always received some managerial support for its contribution to the promotion of employee compliance, it is not, as we have already noted, the open, high-trust, problem-solving relationship which for so many managements would be the ideal. To be sure, negotiating relationships vary widely and few are conducted at an extremity of bitter distrust. But few occupy the other extreme either: indeed the participants in a fully open, high-trust, problem-solving relationship do not see themselves, and are not seen by others, as being in a bargaining situation. Such a pattern is rare, however, as between management and lower-level employees and their representatives. Even in the most cooperative of management/union or management/work-group bargaining relationships there is some irreducible minimum of wary mutual inspection, screening of communication and calculated measuring of specific obligations. These are the dimensions of distrust, and they constitute that failure of full integration which has proved so stubbornly irremediable under the numerous strategies applied by management over the past century.

The future would seem to offer little comfort for those managements still hoping for this full integration. There is no sign that independent trade unionism and collective bargaining are losing their appeal for wage- and salary-earners. In Britain the movement towards union organisation among white-collar employees, which shows signs of intensifying rather than abating, suggests that low-trust attitudes and the ability to express them in behaviour are spreading vertically up the hierarchy to touch, in some cases, even middle-management ranks. On present showing it would seem that, rather than devote scarce time, energy and resources to pursuing the will-o'-the-wisp of rank-and-file involvement and identification, top management might serve its own interests better by directing thought and creativity towards the development of collective bargaining. For, given our current approach to the division of labour and our current inequalities of status and reward, the relationship between the rank-and-file employee and the company is more likely to be shaped by collective bargaining than by management's attempts to integrate him into its own purposes, attitudes and values. A strategy for 'management by agreement' along these lines has recently been expounded by McCarthy and Ellis (see Further Reading).

It is probably safe to say that this will seem to many managers a highly pessimistic forecast. Does it not suggest that management's powers of leadership and command will become increasingly frustrated by collective employee pressures, and that it will have to abandon all hope of inspiring its labour force with a sense of common purpose? And is this not a defeatist, restricted and uncreative role to hold out for management? To examine these arguments requires us to recall some earlier points and propositions.

Embodied in such reactions as these are (1) a refusal to face the implications of extreme division of labour as applied under our present social system; (2) a failure to grasp that major changes are taking place in attitudes towards authority and command; (3) an inadequate definition of leadership; and (4) an assumption that negotiation invariably means merely 'splitting the difference' – an assumption which fails to understand the creative opportunities available to negotiators in designing new syntheses which enlarge the benefits available to both parties. All these points need closer examination.

The first refers to the persistent belief, examined at length in this book, that the rank-and-file employee in the modern large-scale organisation, performing only a humble role and subject to greatly inferior treatment, can yet be induced by suitable personnel policies to identify with the company and offer the appropriate moral involvement. It has been argued here that the many diverse strategies used by management in pursuit of this belief have not yielded notable evidence of success. There are many signs that the typical large-scale organisation does not command the moral adhesion of large proportions of its rank and file, however firmly attached to it they may remain for reasons of self-interested expediency.

The second point relates to the fact that traditional or automatic deference to established authority is shrinking fast. In religious hierarchies, universities, schools and the family, those subject to authority are increasingly disposed to question the fiats of their masters and to evaluate those fiats in the light of their own interests, beliefs or values. Industry could hardly expect to escape this intensification of the 'challenge from below', for the rank-and-file thrust towards collective bargaining preceded – in Britain – even the achievement of political rights through the franchise. Here we may recapitulate some earlier propositions couched in the language of legitimacy. To the extent that men accept as right and proper the rules and decisions of those in command over them they may be said to legitimise them, and this is the basis of willing compliance. To the extent that they do not, their masters normally feel constrained to pressure them (and in the last resort coerce them) into forced compliance. Hence our reference earlier to the twin strategies of consent and coercion. But the coercion strategy suffers the disadvantages of requiring an adequate power superiority and of generating the negative consequences which we have seen management usually anxious if possible to avoid.

Most fundamental for our present argument is the fact that rising aspirations and increasing self-confidence in their own claims are prompting the rank and file to mobilise and assert their collective power with increasing emphasis. These social changes greatly intensify the pressures on higher authority to develop methods of so-called man-management which reduce the need to exercise direct and coercive power. For the greater the extent to which the rank and file are able to mobilise collective power against certain management decisions, the more management would be constrained, if it relied on coercion, to draw upon its own great reserves of power in order to get its own way. The scale of conflict would become greatly enlarged, and with it the negative consequences referred to. We have seen that in trying to escape this predicament management has directed much effort to a search for ways of integrating the rank and file into its own structure of purposes and values. To this end it has sought to arouse in employees a consciousness of participating in a high-trust team relationship of common purpose with the upper ranks of the hierarchy. This endeavour it has tended to define as one of the central expressions of managerial leadership. We have explored, however, those structural features of large-scale industrial organisation which dispose so many members of the rank and file to read managerial purposes and values as divergent in some respects from their own. Against this stubborn obstacle successive waves of leadership endeavour have beaten largely in vain.

Only relatively recently have a few managements been prepared to consider that their central strategy may need to be that of 'negotiated collaboration'. This comprises a number of elements:

(a) there is full acceptance of the pluralist view that the modern industrial organisation has to be seen not as a team but as a coalition of groups making different types of contribution, having different perceptions of the organisation and the wider society, and conscious to some extent of pursuing different interests;

(b) it embodies the opinion that these differences are beyond any likelihood of being assimilated by means of personal leadership and appropriate rallying cries into a common structure of purposes and values determined by top management;

(c) it eschews any hope of imposing such a structure by coercive power, on the grounds that the degree of coercion now required would involve management itself in losses on a scale which it must try to avoid;

(d) the conclusion is drawn that management must put the emphasis on negotiating the terms of collaboration between itself and the various groups.

There is recognition – and here we come to our third point – that to see leadership only in terms of rallying, and offering personal inspiration to, a unified team is too narrow and restricted a definition of that function. In the context of the modern industrial organisation, leadership can take the form of promoting a joint search for that highest negotiated reconciliation of divergent interests (as perceived by the parties) which secures that all participants are conscious of making a net gain. This implies the possibility inherent in the fourth point – that negotiations between groups conscious of divergent interests can be something more than a quest for that 'splitting of the difference' which is usually thought of as the essence of compromise. It can be a creative process resulting in new dispositions and arrangements of technology, organisation, work definitions and pay systems which leave all parties aware of having secured more of what they want from the work situation. Here we have not a compromise but a new synthesis.

The defeatism and pessimism read by some managers into the proposition that negotiated collaboration is increasingly likely to be their central labour strategy are therefore hardly justified. The demands that such a strategy will make upon their creativity, ingenuity, analytical skill and negotiating techniques lift it far above the quality and insight manifested by the panaceas offered them in the past. Any lack of enthusiasm for the prospect can no doubt be attributed to the fact that it invites management to scale down severely – even abandon – what hopes it may cherish of winning over the rank and file to a high-trust, problem-solving, team relationship. A full and complete acceptance of the strategy described here implies acknowledgement that the shortfall in employee integration must be reckoned a permanent, built-in feature of the relationship. To recommend it is therefore to suggest that management recognise as a fact of life a degree of disaffection among its rank and file. By this is meant, as we have already had occasion to emphasise, not necessarily a state of open warfare but one in which the rank and file regard themselves, on certain issues, as independently organised against management in the sense of being disposed to offer a wary inspection of management proposals from a standpoint of divergent interests and values.

For managements still convinced of the possibility of using personal leadership and other integrational techniques to inspire rank-and-file employees with dedication and commitment this recommendation may indeed appear defeatist. Yet argument by such managements that collective bargaining contributes nothing to the process of evoking positive rank-and-file involvement could hardly be regarded as relevant, for in large-scale organisations there has been little evidence of management's ability to evoke it even in the absence of collective bargaining. Neither can they deny that collective bargaining can often contribute a great deal to that other, less ambitious, quest of management: the search for willing compliance which falls well short of moral involvement but nevertheless offers obedience to organisational rules and acceptance of managerial policies. Needless to say, these views have failed to convince many employers and managements over the years. This leads us towards a fuller consideration of the different responses found on both sides of industry to the institution of collective bargaining.

COLLECTIVE BARGAINING: A STANDARD MODEL

For purposes of analysis we may construct a standard model of collective bargaining which is intended not as a description of any particular reality but as a reference point for further discussion. As we proceed it will become evident that our explorations have moved full circle to take up again the themes touched on in the first chapter.

The standard model is grounded firmly on the explicit or implicit acceptance by both negotiating parties of the pluralistic conception of the organisation. The working assumption is made that, on the basis of an approximate parity of power, bargaining representatives conclude collective agreements which can rightly claim observance by those covered, not only for reasons of their own expediency but also because a moral obligation bears upon the parties to any agreement or contract which has been fairly and honourably negotiated free of duress. Our standard model also includes the notion of 'mutual survival'. Each side has, at any one time, a conception of certain entrenched rights which underpin a definition of its own functions, well-being and development, and these rights are recognised by the other. Thus management has, at any one time, a certain view as to those categories of decision-making which should be reserved for its own prerogative, as against those in which it is proper for unions and work-groups to demand participation, and this view is shared by the unions and work-groups themselves. Both parties therefore agree on how they define the frontiers of control and influence.

This agreement has obvious implications for the sense of security enjoyed by the parties and conversely for the degree of vigilant hostility they feel it necessary to deploy against each other. Management feels able to participate in collective bargaining and to afford the employee collective the necessary facilities and even encouragement, confident that no attack is contemplated on those areas of decision-making which it currently sees as defining its own autonomous managerial function and prerogative. On the basis of this confidence it tolerates the collective's challenge to its authority within the agreed range of negotiable issues, and tolerates too the fact that within this range the collective presents itself to employees as a rival focus of leadership and loyalty. Conversely, the collective does not examine every turn of events from a stance of deep suspicion that management will resent and regard as illegitimate its presence in the organisation and will seek to exploit every opportunity to oppose and undermine that presence. Given this confidence that management fully legitimises its functions within the agreed range, the collective feels able to be more open and flexible in its communications and policies than if it were to feel constantly under threat of managerial attack, subversion and distrust.

A further feature of the standard model is that, within the agreed area of joint regulation, neither side persists in claims that are found intolerable by the other. It would clearly be possible for either side to try to enforce demands on which no compromise proved possible – a demand by the union, for example, that wages be doubled, or by management that wages remain constant for a period of years in the face of rising prices. Under our standard model, however, the aspirations asserted by the parties through the bargaining machinery always prove ultimately susceptible of negotiated compromise.

Given these conditions, the participants in our notional model find themselves able to construct and operate joint procedures of negotiation and dispute-settlement. In so doing they demonstrate that within the management/employee relationship there are areas of dispute but also substantial areas of agreement. Management acknowledges that the union has proper and legitimate functions within the organisation and that these include mobilising employees to challenge its prerogative in respect of certain categories of decision. But equally important, the union concedes that management has proper and legitimate functions that include the exercise of decision-making prerogatives over a wide range of issues which the union does not currently choose to dispute. This makes possible – though of course does not guarantee – a system of dual loyalties among employees by which they are conscious of ties to both company and union which coexist and need not be in conflict.

These features demonstrate that under the standard model of collective bargaining the employee collective accommodates to the existing system of hierarchy, division of labour, and authority relations. Management's role is certainly modified in ways which are important for those subject to its rule, but the essential features of the work situation and the management/employee relationship remain the same, with rank-and-file labour viewed as a commodity, allocated to fragmented and closely-controlled low-discretion work, and subject to inferior rewards, status and respect. Under the standard model the collective aims to improve its members' position marginally along a number of these dimensions, particularly money rewards, but does not aspire to changes of such magnitude as could convincingly be portrayed as a qualitative transformation of the system.

DIVERGENCE FROM THE STANDARD: MANAGEMENT AND THE UNITARY FRAME OF REFERENCE

Having sketched the principal features of our notional picture we can now use it as a standard by which to measure the widely diverse situations found in real life. Some could be found which approximate closely to the model. Many others would reveal degrees of divergence from it which might not, however, strike us as so significant as to call for different categories of description. But there would certainly be some situations which diverged so significantly as to dispose us to look for new categories. Two extreme cases of this kind will now be examined. Both have already emerged in other contexts during the earlier exposition. One represents the extreme situation where management totally fails to observe the behaviour patterns described in our standard model. The other points to a similar failure by the employee collective.

The word 'failure' in this context does not necessarily imply that the party in question is *trying* to practise the appropriate behaviours but is not succeeding. To be sure, in this sphere of human action as in all others, men may aim at certain standards yet fail through ignorance, foolishness or lack of foresight. But the possibility also exists that the failure is intentional, that the behaviours in question are not being followed because the party concerned is not pursuing the goals for which they are appropriate. Here we need to register those situations which diverge fundamentally from our notional standard for the reason that management rejects the whole collective bargaining relationship. By its behaviour it demonstrates that it regards the employee collective as having no legitimate functions which involve it in challenging managerial prerogative in any area of decision-making whatever, or in presenting to employees a rival focus of leadership and loyalty which interposes itself between them and management. Refusing thereby to concede any legitimacy to the collective, it remains alert to any opportunity to undermine its position in the organisation or weaken its appeal to employees.

Such a stance is likely to derive from the view that the organisation must be maintained as a unitary structure with but one source of authority and leadership and but one focus of loyalty. Here we have in extreme form the determination to use power to prevent or minimise any union threat to the total integration of the organisation. The union is apt to be seen as a purely external, self-seeking force trying to assert itself into an otherwise integrated and unified system. Success in excluding or severely weakening it is thought to preserve those ties through which management exerts its full prerogative and employees offer their undivided loyalty.

This is not necessarily, from management's point of view, a mistaken formula. If the union has secured no more than a toehold in the organisation and the labour force as a whole remains relatively docile and quiescent, there may be no obvious reason why management should lay itself open to union interference and collective bargaining. Free to regulate terms and conditions of employment and administer its policies unchallenged, it may well see nothing but gain in taking active steps to maintain this situation by resisting the union presence. Such a strategy may enjoy considerable success when conducted within the context of a paternalistic family concern, or a plant that is geographically isolated, or a company whose policy combines non-unionism with the payment of wages well above the rates prevalent in the locality.

The balance of advantages may look very different, of course, if the spirit of collective challenge among some or all of the various occupational groups becomes so strong as to be a significant impediment to management's bureaucratic regulation of labour conditions and its exercise of prerogative in day-to-day business. Given the will and ability of work-groups to contest decisions and impose costs on management unless it makes some accommodation to their needs and aspirations, the principle of enlightened self-interest may come to point, for management, in the direction of recognising the union stake in decision-making and seeing systematic collective bargaining as the best means of promoting that compliance which it now finds problematical.

This is not to suggest, however, that this issue, or any other issue for that matter, is necessarily resolved by the calm application of sweet reason and rational appraisal of costs and benefits. We are dealing here with power relations, and men with power are apt to value it for its own sake as well as for what they can do with it. In other words, power may yield them intrinsic satisfactions as well as instrumental usefulness. Where this is the case the issue of whether to yield to union power pressures for participation in certain types of decision-making may well be partly determined by managerial responses which have little to do with calm appraisals of whether union participation will or will not serve management interests. Counsel may be darkened by a primitive impulse to prevent any encroachment on personal prerogatives. Status considerations may also play a part. Resentment at being called upon to explain and justify one's actions and negotiate on them with persons of inferior occupational and social status was a common response among earlier generations of employers, and although few managers today would admit to a sentiment so unhelpful to public relations, the possibility that it survives in some quarters must be borne in mind.

Recognition of these impulses which can prejudice management's rational appraisal of the costs and benefits of union recognition and collective bargaining may have a wider application. Located on the continuum between the standard model and a total assertion of the unitary perspective are many situations which share some of the characteristics of both. Management may be prepared to engage in collective bargaining provided the employee collective confines its challenge within the limits found convenient by management, moderates the size of its claims to a level which enables management to settle for acceptable compromises, and contributes to the handling of grievances and disputes a spirit of give and take which fully recognises the principle of mutual survival. But the employee collective may not observe these terms. It may on occasion press upon the relevant limits in ways which for management reopen the whole question of the value of collective bargaining. Clearly there may enter into these management responses the same primitive resentments relating to power and status which we have already noted. They help to explain the sudden emotional flare-up which sometimes aggravates the problems of a tricky bargaining situation.

We see here, then, a scale of management attitudes towards collective bargaining ranging from total acceptance (given the preconditions) to total rejection, with many companies occupying positions between these extremes and perhaps changing their position according to shifts in employee aspirations or changes in company circumstances.

DIVERGENCE FROM THE STANDARD: THE WORK-GROUP AND THE RADICAL FRAME OF REFERENCE

The same range of possibilities exists for the employee collective. It may, as we have seen, share with management a definition of the entrenched rights of both parties which enables them to conduct their relations in a spirit of mutual survival and therefore mutual security. At the other extreme, we may imagine a collective – perhaps a totally disaffected work-group – acting in a manner which allows the inference to be drawn that it has completely withdrawn legitimation from management and concedes no right on management's part to discharge its present functions within the existing institutional framework of industry. To be sure, management may be able, perhaps at some loss to itself, to coerce the group into a forced compliance. But the essential conditions for a stable negotiated peace are not present. The employee collective does not offer that contribution which, along with the corresponding contribution from management, creates the reciprocity of mutual survival.

In the absence of this reciprocity, negotiation as normally understood is not possible. Management finds that the give and take which it sees as normally playing a major part in relationships with rank and file is not present. The collective appears to press every tactical advantage to the utmost, to resist the notion of mutual concession, to work actively against the promotion of mutual trust. This is, of course, simply a mirror image of the behaviour manifested by a management which refuses to concede legitimacy to the union presence. Coming from an employee collective it represents a total distrust of management which can spring either from experience in the particular company or industry concerned or from a generalised ideological rejection of the whole institutional framework of industry *and* society. At this point we return full circle to the theme with which we began: the contrasting images which different men and groups have of society, and in particular the radical stance which withholds legitimacy from management functions as at present socially defined.

But just as management attitudes usually lie between the extremes, so do those of employee collectives. While coming nowhere near denying management all legitimacy, the collective may yet wish to challenge managerial prerogative on issues which lie beyond the limits which management seeks to impose on its participation. Faced with continued exclusion from these issues, which management insists on retaining solely in its own hands, or perhaps grudgingly conceded a limited participation which management seeks always to restrict and even reduce, the collective finds reason for distrust which may either coexist with mutual confidence on other issues or gradually spread until it permeates the whole relationship.

THE APPEAL TO GOVERNMENT AND THE POLITICAL
POWER STRUCTURE

As these considerations show, the standard model of collective bargaining sketched earlier is useful only as a reference point to help us gauge the relative presence or absence of certain selected qualities in real-life situations. Perhaps few relationships between management and employee collective embody the full reciprocity of mutual acceptance displayed by the standard model. But the discussion has shown that in all situations where collective bargaining persists there is *some* body of shared ideas and values. Bargaining institutions prosper only when management recognises the collective's claim that it has a right to exist, when the collective acknowledges that management must be allowed functions it currently deems crucial, when both can agree that their relationship shall continue, and when both subscribe to certain procedures, modes and values through which to conduct this relationship.

The prevalence of such situations in our society should perhaps reassure the fearful, though doubtless disappoint the revolutionaries with its implication that we are still far short of that anarchy so widely seen as characterising Britain's present condition. There are few signs yet of any widespread disposition to challenge management's hierarchical structures with their extreme division of labour, unsatisfying work routines, subordination and control, and highly unequal rewards, status and respect, though there are certainly visible on managerial horizons a few faint smudges which may prove to be growing clouds. These we shall examine later. Meanwhile it is apparent that the institution of collective bargaining itself can still generate social tensions. Here and there managements try to resist it altogether and evoke deep frustration among unions seeking recognition as negotiating agents. Elsewhere managements may accept bargaining about pay but resist its extension, say, to disciplinary codes. Conversely, employee collectives can arouse a high pitch of hostility from management by pressing unacceptably hard with respect to both the range and the intensity of their claims, flouting agreed procedures for handling those claims, and manifesting too little of the spirit of give and take deemed desirable in day-to-day business.

Each side looks round for allies, and since the greatest potential ally is the state there develops the likelihood of appeals to governments for legislative support. Unions seek legislation which would help them, for example, in securing recognition from resistant managements; managements seek legislation which would help them in curbing those forms and degrees of collective pressure which give them special difficulty. Expressed in this way the position of the parties may seem agreeably symmetrical. The two major interest groups of capital and labour appear to have equal access to governments for supportive legislation and, given the political pendulum which seems to award its favours alternately between the major parties, an approximation to rough justice is assured over the long term. We may draw upon the analysis of the first chapter, however, to argue that this appearance of symmetry is illusory, just as the whole notion of a power-balance is illusory. The legislative struggle takes place over measures designed to strengthen or weaken the ability of organised labour to challenge management only at the margins of the institutional structure of industry. As we have seen, the management/union struggle is not about such fundamentals of that structure as hierarchy, subordination, extreme division of labour, labour as commodity, and massive inequalities of treatment. These are – as yet – almost universally accepted by the rank and file in the sense of being seen, apparently, as inevitable and beyond any power of theirs to contest. Certainly we are all urged by a multiplicity of conditioning influences to see such features as right and proper, unavoidable, beyond the reach of human choice to change.

The struggle therefore takes place at the margins of this structure on issues which seem to employee collectives to be within their capacity to affect. How big the wage, how long the shift, what length the holiday, how heavy the work stint, on what conditions the job transfer, under what arrangements the redundancy – such are the usual categories of decision-making in which employee collectives seek a foothold. And it is legislation designed to influence one way or the other the ability of collectives to participate in *these* decisions which has been the subject of the relevant political struggles as conducted so far in Britain. What have been referred to here as the fundamentals of the institutional framework have remained untouched. The superior power of those concerned to preserve them has always been amply sufficient to daunt even such members of strong Labour governments as might cherish aspirations towards radical change. Thus the political struggle, like the industrial struggle, has so far been conducted largely at the margins of the system, and the reason for this has been the power of those individuals and groups whose interests, objectives or values are served by confining contention to the margins and preventing any more basic challenge.

Here we see at work the least visible and least discussed yet the most important and most significant characteristic of power – the part it plays in defining the issues and problems which come up for private and public contention and debate. Men conscious of relative weakness in a power relationship usually see as a waste of time and resources any aspirations which seem far beyond their capacity to realise. Similarly, most of those who shape and conduct public discussion through the media of radio, press and television are conscious of pressures to seem 'realistic', 'relevant' and 'topical', and are aware too, no doubt, of the influential disfavour apt to be directed at those who encourage 'destructive' and 'irresponsible' attacks by 'extremists' upon the fundamentals of the system. Thus they, too, play their part in determining the limits and nature of the public debate, thereby socialising us in what to see as the important and relevant issues and problems. For all that they pride themselves on their impartiality, it is an impartiality only between parties contesting issues at the margins of the system, not between parties contesting the assumptions, merits and values of the system as a whole. To exemplify the difference we may imagine a parson who is concerned about pilfering from church fund boxes being told by a television interviewer that, in order to preserve the absolute impartiality of debate, the spokesman who has just recommended stealing the entire contents will be followed by one who will recommend that pilferers remove no more than half.

In many subtle as well as not-so-subtle ways, therefore, the power structure operates not only, and not even mainly, by determining the outcome of such conflicts as do occur, but also by determining what kinds of conflicts do *not* occur. And in terms of maintaining in recognisable shape the basic fundamentals of the system it is the latter function which is the more crucial. Consequently, in trying to make an overall assessment of the workings of society and how different groups fare within it, it is as important to identify those issues which politics and collective bargaining do not deal with as to identify those with which they do.

THE ROLE OF TRADE UNIONISM AND COLLECTIVE BARGAINING IN SOCIETY

When we appraise the situation in this light, collective bargaining emerges as a process through which employee collectives aspire, not to transform their work situation, but to bend it somewhat in their favour. This limited and pragmatic purpose expresses what they currently see as a realistic adaptation to the facts of power, what they are induced by a multitude of influences to regard as a legitimate aspiration on their part, and what degree of self-confidence they feel in making this or that specific demand.

It is a process often misunderstood by conservatives and radicals alike. The former have sometimes seen it as a threat to the social order; the latter have sometimes derided it as shadow-boxing which, far from changing anything, serves only to prop up an unjust system. It is important, even at the cost of some recapitulation, to identify what is, and is not, valid in this particular radical position. Any wholesale disparagement of the part which can be played by collective bargaining in the work experience of those who feel the need for it reveals nothing more edifying than a total lack of insight into the nature of that experience. Perhaps those who press an extreme view here are not open to the sort of evidence which demonstrates the value that members so often place on their collective – such as the strong resistance they normally offer, given the chance, to any attack on its existence. Yet the limits to the role of collective bargaining have been revealed by our exploration of its very nature and of the values and assumptions on which it rests. It has survived because each party has conceded certain entrenched rights to the other – which for the employee collective has meant submitting to the institutional structure that decrees, among other things, extreme subordination and inferior treatment for its members.

The importance of the negotiation method for the collective's leaders in securing concessions has impelled them to propagate among their members, explicitly and implicitly, the values and assumptions which inform and support that method. Rank and file, as well as leaders, have had to offer a general acceptance of its codes of behavioural restraints and its recognition of what are currently to be seen 'realistically' as negotiable as against non-negotiable issues. Thus we have a situation in which the widespread and influential institutions of trade unionism and collective bargaining figure among those social forces which, far from stimulating rank-and-file employees into ever-rising aspirations and ever-sharpening challenges to managerial prerogative and authority, have served rather to contain them and confine them within those limits currently deemed appropriate for the continuance of the negotiation method. Trade unions have helped, in other words, to socialise their members in what it is sensible to demand of their work situation and in the methods (agreed with management) by which those demands should be pursued. Needless to say, the directions of influence have also operated in the reverse direction. Trade union members draw upon many other sources besides the union in fashioning their aspirations and their view of society, industry and work, and there are many formal and informal processes through which they communicate these aspirations and views to their leaders. Union officers and shop stewards are therefore right to stress that the ends they pursue and the means they employ to pursue them must always be responsive to membership wishes. But this is only half the story, for the union itself and its associated practices, methods and procedures help to shape membership conceptions of both ends and means.

Here we begin to draw close to what is valid in the radical critique of pluralist interpretations of how Western society works. It will be recalled that, starting from the assumption of an approximate power balance between the major interest groups, these interpretations present party-political democracy, trade unionism and collective bargaining as introducing into the system a degree of equity with respect to decision-making sufficient to render it tolerably fair and thereby deserving of respect and support. How many rank-and-file employees would find this picture convincing we do not know. What we do know, with respect to the work situation, is that the institutions of trade unionism and collective bargaining help to marshal them into patterns of aspirations and behaviour which, on the whole, support rather than challenge the fundamental structural features of the *status quo*. This, then, is how the radical critique perceives collective bargaining – as a process by which the rank and file, inferior in power, status and treatment, are allowed to press for marginal improvements in their lot on condition that they leave unchallenged those structural features of the system which perpetuate their inferiority. They are then urged to see the process as affording them parity with management and as thereby justifying the demand that they offer moral adhesion to the system as a whole. From the radical perspective, then, the institutions of collective bargaining and the social propositions which support and derive from it are in no sense neutral or balanced, but are heavily weighted in favour of the *status quo*.

Are there, however, any signs of change in the industrial relations scene which might affect the ways in which collective bargaining is viewed and utilised by relevant groups? Social prediction is notoriously more fallible and misleading than prediction in the world of natural science, where all the relevant variables are susceptible of being identified and measured. What will be attempted in the next chapter is not so much prediction as a discussion of certain signs, symptoms and apparent trends, and the possible consequences if they were to develop further. The vulnerability of this kind of exercise is apparent. Some or all of them may prove in the coming decades to have been transitory and to show no development or significance. Alternatively their effects may be countered or overborne by other developments which we are not yet noticing or regarding as significant. Such uncertainties cannot, however, exempt us from the constant struggle to understand our world, and this means we must do our best with what evidence we have.

Further Reading

BAKKE, E. W. *Mutual Survival: The Goal of Unions and Management*. New York: Harper and Bros., 1946.

BEYNON, H. *Working for Ford*. Harmondsworth: Penguin Books, 1973.

BLACKBURN, R., COCKBURN, A. (eds) *The Incompatibles: Trade Union Militancy and the Consensus*. Harmondsworth: Penguin Books, 1967.

FLANDERS, A. (ed.) *Collective Bargaining*. Harmondsworth: Penguin Books, 1969.

HYMAN, R. *Strikes*. London: Fontana/Collins, 1972.

MCCARTHY, W. E. J., ELLIS, N. D. *Management by Agreement*. London: Hutchinson, 1973.

MILIBAND, R. *The State in Capitalist Society*. London: Weidenfeld and Nicolson, 1969.

THOMAS, J. M., BENNIS, W. G. (eds) *Management of Change and Conflict*. Harmondsworth: Penguin Books, 1972.

7. Participation and the Status Quo

MANAGERIAL PREROGATIVE AND ITS CHANGING
DEFINITION

We have seen that whether collective bargaining maintains
ordered relations free of prolonged breakdowns and recurrent
disruptions depends on there being (a) a high degree of con-
gruence between the views of the two parties as to what categories of decisions are to be seen as negotiable and what as
non-negotiable, and (b) a closeness between the claims, aspirations or policies of the parties with respect to negotiable issues
sufficient to make possible those agreed compromises or syntheses which maintain uninterrupted working.

Preceding chapters have argued that capital and labour cannot convincingly be seen as equal parties, each influenced
neither directly nor indirectly by the power of the other, freely
choosing just what issues they would prefer to negotiate about
and what practical aspirations to entertain in respect of each
issue. Labour has been described here as being strongly dominated along both these dimensions by the greatly superior
power of capital.

But the history of collective bargaining shows that, faced
with the growing will, ability and self-confidence of employee
collectives in mobilising and deploying their strength, employers
and managers have considered it judicious to relax their ideas
on prerogative and have not suffered a collapse of their functions, status and privileges as a consequence. Earlier generations of entrepreneurs could fall into outraged fury at the
suggestion that they might discuss wage rates with an outside
union 'agitator' or even with an abashed cap-in-hand deputa-
tion of their own workmen, regarding this as, among other
things, an intolerable slight to their social status. But experience

convinced them that, given the conditions we have noted, it need be neither demeaning nor economically crippling to live with the unions and collective bargaining. Indeed some came to see them as offering positive advantages. And as time passed many felt it prudent to heed other signs of social change. Improved living standards were filtering down to the rank and file; they were given the franchise; they raised their status and aspirations. Increasingly they asserted themselves as citizens who could not be denied, in their work situation, some version of the rights they now enjoyed in the political field. The middle-class sympathy and support once freely offered to employers who openly attacked the unions and collective bargaining became somewhat less reliable. And while there were always those for whom this shift in social values was a matter of indifference, many considered it judicious to change with the times and behave accordingly. Thus what had once seemed an insolent challenge to employer prerogatives and status came to be seen as standard practice which had to be lived with and made the best of. As they became increasingly habituated to the practice over the years, employers and managers found it easier to keep their tempers provided union demands observed the conditions discussed earlier.

These developments demonstrate that the conception held by employers at any one time as to the extent of their prerogative is not a constant in some presumed pattern of human nature, nor yet a fixed and unchanging element in their definition of the management role. Rather is it an interpretation which, besides varying according to how they respond individually to challenges to their power and status, can be affected by changes in the values of social groups whose goodwill and support they prefer not to forgo. And it is clear that the latter can affect the former. Men may react emotionally when their expectations are violated or frustrated. But they develop these expectations as members of a society, and may change them under the influence of shifts in social values. And when expectations change, events which previously triggered off anger and resistance may do so no longer. Present-day management is far less likely than the early entrepreneurs to offer vehement and emotional resistance to an employee demand for negotiation about pay. The logical implication is clear. Perhaps, given further changes in social values, it could become habituated to negotiating about issues which it currently regards as wholly within its prerogative.

Care must be taken, however, to avoid over-simple projections. There could prove to be items in both the 'technical' and 'business' categories which continue to be seen by management as so central to its function, status and rewards that its resistance to negotiation on these issues stiffens progressively as such core activities are approached. Feeling could be so intense as to rule out any possibility of being influenced by changes in values in the wider society should these show signs of moving in labour's favour. Instead, management might devote considerable resources to attempts at securing that the predominant values in society did not move against them in this way. Such attempts would (on the assumption that they stopped short of state-supported violence) probably take the form of ideological and propagandist campaigns designed to convince as many as possible (a) that the latest proposed encroachments on their prerogative would destroy management as a specialist function serving the public interest, and (b) that the new demands were therefore essentially 'political' in a subversive sense which called for the mobilisation of the sane, loyal elements in society.

What we are now considering, therefore, is the possibility that employee collectives, given increasing strength, rising aspirations and growing confidence in asserting them, might be found pressing hard against the defences of what management uncompromisingly defined as sacred ground. In such circumstances there is a strong possibility that employers would condemn this union or work-group pressure as fundamentally political in nature. This brings us to the distinction between 'industrial' and 'political' issues: an important one calling for closer examination.

INDUSTRIAL AND POLITICAL ISSUES

The distinction between industrial and political issues is a key feature of Britain's industrial relations system, and constitutes another of the joint understandings which comprise the pluralist philosophy informing relationships between the organised

forces of employers, trade unions and the party-political structure. These two categories are deemed each to have their own
appropriate procedures of resolution and their own appropriate
arenas within which the procedures are conducted. The procedures appropriate to industrial issues are of course collective
bargaining, conciliation and arbitration, followed, if these fail,
by the strike (or lockout), the overtime ban, the go-slow, the
work-to-rule and similar forms of pressure. The arena is industry
itself, as represented by the organised forces of the employer or
employers and the union or unions, along with such services as
may be forthcoming from the government department concerned with these matters. The political arena constituted by
parliament discusses these conflicts defined as industrial –
definitions about which there is considerable agreement between employers, unions and the political parties – only when
they cause widespread disruption. Even then, Labour members
of parliament ordinarily tread as gingerly as do their Conservative counterparts, directing their attention less to the supposed
rights and wrongs of the conflict than to criticism of the government's action – or inaction – in the matter. The ostensible
principle to which all wish to appear to be paying deference
is that of saying nothing which might make the situation
worse.

We may suppose the Parliamentary Labour Party's motivation here to spring from two major considerations. The first is
no doubt an anxiety to appear 'responsible', alert to 'the
national interest', and unfettered by exclusive ties to the trade
unions. The other is likely to be a general disposition to avoid
interfering in what is deemed the unions' industrial business
unless specifically invited. The Parliamentary Labour Party is
under a strong incentive to observe this convention, for it can
then demand reciprocity from the trade unions in leaving
political issues to be handled by political methods within the
political arena. The conviction is widespread and emphatic
within the Parliamentary Party that the unions should not use
weapons fashioned for the industrial struggle, like the strike, in
the pursuit of political ends, which should be reserved to the
procedure and protocol of the Commons and the Lords. Labour
politicians are no less protective of parliamentary supremacy
than their Conservative counterparts.

Most union leaders show no unwillingness to respect this convention, for they too have their reciprocal expectations. But, like the politicians, their interest in respecting it is twofold. Just as Labour politicians see it as possibly damaging for them if they obtrude their political role too partisanly into industrial conflicts, so union leaders see as possibly dangerous the deployment of their industrial battalions on the field of political conflict. For the politicians, the threat is to their claim to be a 'national' party; for the union leaders, to their rights and facilities as industrial negotiators. Our concern here being with the industrial field, it is the latter we need to examine more closely. Why should union leaders see danger for what has become their central function in our society, namely collective bargaining, in using their industrial strength for political purposes? In trying to answer this question we shall find ourselves pursuing different implications of the word 'political', one with particular relevance for their dealings with politicians, the other for their dealings with management.

In the first case, the unions' deployment of their industrial power to pressure or coerce the politicians would bring them into conflict with men who could, if they chose, use the legislative (and in the last resort, coercive) processes of the state to limit union rights and strength. There would be much support for this response from those alarmed at the prospect of the country's economic life being disrupted by industrial stoppages in pursuit of political purposes which they deem should receive expression only within the appropriate political institutions. If we ask who benefits most from this arrangement it will seem a reasonable assumption that the exclusion of the unions' industrial power from the arena of party politics will particularly favour the more privileged sections of society. Political issues about which the unions felt strongly enough to use their industrial strength would be unlikely to command the sympathies of the well-to-do, who must therefore be reckoned to have a special interest in the convention we are examining. However, the unions would not support such a convention unless it yielded them too (given their perceptions, values and objectives) some sort of return. And the return here lies in the fact that if the unions abstain from applying their industrial strength to political causes which offend the interests of wealth, power and status, then these in turn will not feel the need to use their great reserves of power to cripple the unions.

On this tacit understanding the unions can grow, thrive and have their being within the circumscribed area of action allowed them. The wealthy and powerful continue to enjoy their privileges, subject to yielding certain concessions which nevertheless leave the essential structure of industry and society intact, while the unions and their members develop a stake in their participatory role as joint decision-makers with management over the limited area covered by collective bargaining. Provided their perceptions, values and objectives undergo no fundamental change, they can find this role sufficiently satisfactory to give them a strong consciousness of having something to lose. They will then assess their strategies and policies by criteria which include the need to avoid weakening, and to ward off any threat to, the institution of collective bargaining. Thus derives the fear that to use extreme industrial weapons against the politicians might bring down upon themselves and upon their functions the wrath of far more powerful sections of society. When used to support this conception, the distinction between political and industrial issues bears an ideological connotation in that it underpins a particular interpretation of the proper role of trade unions in our society – an interpretation which, as we have seen, embodies values and assumptions supportive of the *status quo*.

By this time the reader may be somewhat restless at the preceding references to industrial and political issues on the grounds that no attempt has been made to define them. What makes one issue industrial and another political? There are no objective criteria. Issues have no *intrinsic* quality which lead us to put some in one category and some in the other. The difference simply lies in the methods by which we try to provide for their resolution. Political issues are those we currently handle through the institutions and procedures of national and local party democracy, while industrial issues are those resolved by management, or by unions, or by joint negotiating institutions representative of both.

There is nothing fixed or mutually exclusive about the allocation of issues to these categories. An issue may move from one to the other or finish up in both. It may begin, as in the case of the terms on which men may be declared redundant, by being regarded purely as a matter for decision within industry itself, and later become also a legislative issue at the national political level. In earlier times the determination of wage rates was deemed to be the ultimate prerogative of the state, exercised through annual assessments by the local magistrates with reference to the trades within their area. In the nineteenth century the last remnants of this (doubtless always uncertain) procedure were swept away by the conviction that such decisions must rest solely within industry's own purview. Even when this ideology of *laissez-faire* was enjoying its nineteenth-century apogee, however, governments in Britain were being constrained by the exigencies of opinion and events to legislate certain maxima with respect to working hours. Later came the state concern with factory health, sanitation, industrial injury and wage minima in certain selected industries. The categorisation of what are industrial and what political issues is therefore shifting and conventional. There can be said to exist, at any one time, prevailing views as to which issues ought to belong in which categories, but these views are often contested by groups whose opinions do not currently prevail but may become the standard orthodoxy a few years hence. So nothing about the present categorisation is sacrosanct, and no objective principles can be advanced to support an assertion of this kind.

We can go further, however, than to say that the two categories are conventional and not mutually exclusive. A case can be made that the whole distinction between the industrial and the political now rests on no more than paper-thin foundations, for its basis has been increasingly undermined by forces that have been at work for many years. Over a whole spectrum of issues ranging much wider than those of management/union relations, history has witnessed an increasing interpenetration of these two spheres of activity. Events of the last half-century have demonstrated that the development and exigencies of the modern national and international economy tend to draw the state more and more into active intervention for the purposes of regulating domestic economic affairs, promoting growth and influencing the nation's external trading relations. Increasingly the fortunes of governments are determined by their success (according to prevalent definitions) in monetary and fiscal management, in maintaining growth while containing inflation, and in striving towards economic viability within the world economy. Thus more and more the political levels of decision-making become involved in shaping many of the forces to which industry has to respond or which in some way limit its choices. By the same token, they shape the context within which trade unions operate. The unions cannot but be aware that political decisions can greatly affect what they are able to achieve for their members.

It has always been true, of course, that the state of the law, and how it is moulded by political legislators as well as inter-preted by the courts, establishes a framework within which unions shape their objectives and fashion their methods. But increasingly political decisions affect the economic events to which those objectives and methods are a response. Such deci-sions have a bearing, for example, on the general level of employment, economic activity and demand for labour; on the state of labour markets in particular regions and even particular companies; on monetary and fiscal measures relating to prices and the cost of living; on the issue of expansion or contraction in particular industries; on the location of new economic deve-lopment; and above all (in the form of incomes policy) on the constraints which bear upon unions and employers in their bargaining activities. Increasing awareness of the impact of these decisions upon their functions and achievements is likely increasingly to push the unions into seeking a voice in them. If it makes sense – and is justified by the democratic ethos – for a shop steward, as leader of his work-group, to press for a say in his foreman's decisions about piece-rates, then equal sense and justification would attach to an aspiration by his union to par-ticipate in decisions affecting the conduct and fortunes of the company, the industry, the society in which they are located, and the economic relations between that society and the outside world – all of which bear upon the work experience, well-being, and destinies of the union's membership.

Political decisions and industrial issues being thus inextricably interwoven, unions can only fully apply themselves to the latter by pressing also for admission to the former. Being organisations with the central function of modifying decision-making, they are under pressure to seek out the highest as well as the lowest relevant levels at which this takes place. There is, of course, a litter of consultative and advisory bodies on which trade unionists serve even now and which touch this wider decision-making structure at certain points. But these commit nobody. Events may well push unions into seeking firm commitments from the government with respect to certain strategic areas of policy. Indeed, events may push unions, government and employers into seeking commitments from each other. The likelihood is, therefore, that the distinction between political and industrial issues will make less and less sense as the unions feel the need to bring their pressure-group and negotiating functions to bear upon government decisions which shape the fortunes of their members. And it would be an unwary prophet who asserted that the strike threat and other expressions of industrial strength would never play any part in these processes. Possibilities of conflict would exist over such matters as what issues of high government policy were negotiable, and what the limits of change were for the issues being negotiated. Already, therefore, the assertion that 'the strike weapon must never be used for political purposes' begins to take on a somewhat dated air as a symbol of an epoch when governments were less deeply involved in that arena which engrosses the principal preoccupations and functions of the unions.

POLITICAL ISSUES AND PARTICIPATION

There is, furthermore, another usage of the term 'political' which, like the one just examined, is ideological in its implications and also liable to be overtaken by events in the not too distant future. This usage supports the exclusion of certain types of issue from the bargaining process as conducted within industry itself. We have noted how the standard model of collective bargaining embodies agreed notions as to which issues are negotiable and which are non-negotiable. Issues seen by managements as non-negotiable would be those which seemed to them to introduce a threat to structures and arrangements crucial to their essential functions and well-being (as they define them). A similar definition can be applied to the unions. Any significant encroachment by either side upon these limits creates strains for the relationship until either the initiating party withdraws or the other accepts the new frontiers of joint regulation. In order to strengthen the defences of its own frontier each party is normally ready with a legitimising formula which seeks to mobilise support within society at large. 'Traditional' trade union rights or 'proper' management functions are invoked as essential, integral and legitimate elements in the established social framework. Encroachments on its frontier can then be condemned by the party concerned as subversive. It is a conception which comes far more readily, of course, to the lips of management, for the claims of property, authority and status are integral with the established social order to a degree not shared by the unions. Nevertheless, a sustained and large-scale challenge to existing union functions, from whatever source it came, would certainly be seen by sizeable sections of the population, outside as well as inside the unions, as subversive. In other words, it would be described as political, where the context revealed that the word was intended to have derogatory connotations.

This label is sometimes applied to work-group (or, less often, union) aspirations and claims which press uncomfortably hard upon the frontiers of prerogative as management defines them. As we have seen, these frontiers protect structural arrangements, principles, values and decision-making roles considered essential to managerial functions and privileges, but common also to most economic political and social organisations of any size in our society. Understandably, therefore, management shares with many others the conviction that they are fundamental to the existing social order. Any strong refusal to submit to them is bound to seem 'irresponsible', 'unreasonable' and 'unpatriotic' to those anxious to uphold them. It will also seem 'political'. The charge of being political will always be levelled at those whose aspirations appear to threaten the stability of an established order. The use of the word in a derogatory context therefore serves an ideological purpose. Indeed, in such a context the whole distinction between political and industrial issues is an ideological one, for it serves to discredit those which constitute a challenge to the existing system while tolerating those which do not.

At this stage we can draw from the argument a point relevant to all forms of employee participation in decision-making. We can recognise a distinction between participation activity which is deemed by those in positions of authority to accept the existing system and to work within it, and participation activity which in some respect or another is seen as rejecting the system and seeking to change it. Those who for reasons of personal interest, objectives or values identify with the existing system may tolerate, possibly even welcome, the first. They will certainly oppose the second. Here we establish a link with a point noted earlier. The support offered by management and by those in sympathy with its values and purposes to the notion of participation is never open-ended. It is bounded by the extent to which participation confines its aspirations and pressures within what is currently deemed the essential framework of the prevailing order. The management approach to participation is thus as fully instrumental as the other personnel and labour strategies examined in this book. For all the talk of 'treating people as ends in themselves and no longer as mere means', employee participation can only enjoy management support and encouragement when it takes place on management terms and can be justified in some way or another as ultimately contributing to managerial purposes and values. When, therefore, employee representatives taking part in decision-making come under familiar exhortations to 'Be responsible', 'Be reasonable' or 'Be patriotic', these can often be translated to mean: 'Limit your claims and aspirations to what is compatible with the stability and continuance of prevailing social values, institutions, priorities and arrangements.'

CURRENT ASPIRATIONS AND THE FUTURE

The question which next suggests itself concerns the extent to which we can detect claims and aspirations now being pressed within the industrial participative machinery which do constitute some kind of challenge to the prevailing order. But before we get to grips with this we need to distinguish three different types of challenge. The first is presented by those who, regarding society as unjust and wishing to see it changed in radical and fundamental ways, feel impelled to look for means by which they can help to make existing institutions unworkable. So far as collective bargaining is concerned they may hope to pursue this end by encouraging employee claims and aspirations on issues deemed by management to be non-negotiable, and by encouraging claims and aspirations on issues that *are* negotiable to be pitched so high as to intensify the usual difficulties of compromise. As we have seen, either of these eventualities puts collective bargaining institutions under strain.

The second type of challenge comes from groups who, without any conscious aspiration to change society, simply wish, for example, to improve their own relative position in terms of money or status, enhance their job security, enjoy more fairness and respect in the treatment they receive, secure greater protection against authority, win freedom from being treated as a commodity, have their work made more interesting, or whatever. For all that they have no conscious thought of changing the system, it might be that a condition of their achieving their aims on a permanent and stable basis would be quite significant changes in social values, institutions, objectives or priorities. For example, if a major social group A is permanently to improve its position relatively to major social groups B and C, these must submit to having their position permanently worsened relatively to A. Implicit in such a shift would be changes in valuation and status which, in the terms of the present discussion, must be considered political in nature. If those who offer challenges of this second kind find it useful and convenient, as they well might, to accept the leadership of those seeking to present a challenge of the first kind, a type of situation is likely to emerge which those in authority frequently derogate as politically inspired.

The third type of challenge is of a different order. The two just examined, though different in that the first derives from a conscious political philosophy while the second (despite its political implications) does not, are alike in that the challenge lies in the nature of the claim and is actively willed by those presenting it. The third, however, is largely an unintended consequence of behaviour within a large number of negotiating situations each of which in itself contains no challenge to established priorities, principles or institutions. The threat derives from the stresses imposed on the system when a multiplicity of

groups negotiate wage and salary increases within an inflationary situation. We do not need to assume that trade unions
cause inflation, only to be fairly confident that they aggravate it.
But by far the great majority of union leaders and members do
not will this consequence. They will only a pay increase. Yet
the combined effect of their separate pressures is to produce
severe problems for those seeking to administer and uphold the
system as a whole, problems which throw into some doubt its
continuation in the present form should existing trends continue. These three types of challenge now need to be examined
more closely.

Since those who wish to offer the first are so relatively few,
their only present hope of promoting the unworkability of, and
consequent loss of confidence in, existing institutions lies in
capitalising on the other two. Perhaps one of the most persistent
misjudgements committed by established authority is its exag-
geration of their ability to do this. Radicals and revolutionaries
might well wish they really did enjoy those powers of creating
mass disaffection out of thin air with which they are so freely
credited. Detached observers, however, have often pointed to
the abundant evidence that while those bent on disruption can
often fish successfully in troubled waters they cannot generate
these favourable circumstances wholly by themselves. They can
focus and sharpen grievances, encourage militant rather than
conciliatory means of pursuing them, and place themselves at
the head of aggressive action. They cannot, however, conjure
up a mass grievance where none exists, and far more revolutionary hearts have been broken by rank-and-file indifference
than have been warmed by a militant readiness to take up the
struggle. Even when their troops have followed them on to the
battlefield in pursuit of a bread-and-butter grievance which they
have managed to adorn with the rallying cries of the class war,
they have been mortified to discover that once the bread-and-
butter objective is achieved their army soon melts away, leaving
the ground strewn with abandoned revolutionary banners. But
while established authority often exaggerates the ability of the
militant leader to promote and sustain mass disturbance, there
is probably more substance in the tendency to believe that its
interests would be furthered by eliminating him and (it is hoped)
leaving the rank and file leaderless. Admittedly this too is often

157

questioned by the liberal observer. Experience has shown, he may argue, that a mass grievance is not eliminated by getting rid of the leader who focuses, articulates and organises it. Authority's obsession with his importance merely expresses its need for the self-reassuring belief that basically the rank and file are loyal if gullible, and that only the interfering and often politically motivated firebrand is responsible for the really serious disruption.

These are important elements in any diagnosis, but in themselves they gloss over an important point. To eliminate the leader who is focusing, articulating and organising a grievance may represent for management (as for any other ruler) a considerable gain. Certainly the grievance itself is not thereby eliminated, and another leader may spring forward to fill the gap, more bitter and desperate than his predecessor. But the grievance has to be of great intensity to ensure this, and in many situations of a less extreme temper the supply of those prepared to incur the potential strains and penalties of leading a campaign against superior power is strictly limited. Even in the absence of leadership, however, will not the grievance manifest itself in a variety of covert ways no less disagreeable to management? It may or it may not; management may believe it can control these alternative expressions or consider them less costly. There is no intention here of supporting any general proposition that management's best policy is always to try to eliminate the troublesome leader. Judged by long-term criteria which take the widest possible view of costs this may often be a mistake. But there are probably situations where it is not *necessarily* true that for management to suppress an aggressive and disaffected employee leadership does managerial interests more harm than good. Any such assumption is a liberal illusion.

Against the background of these observations on the part played by the first type of challenge, we turn to the second. It will be recalled that we are interested in possibilities with respect to claims and aspirations which could represent a challenge to the prevailing system. A brief recapitulation of those structural features specially significant for assessing the work situation of the industrial rank and file will serve to suggest some such possibilities. Employee groups could conceivably become concerned, for example, to improve their pay, status and general treatment relatively to those enjoyed by top management and other favoured groups, thereby pressing for a more egalitarian society. They might seek to destroy or weaken the concept of labour as a commodity, by which it is taken for granted that they can be hired or discarded as management interests demand, and insist instead that productive exigencies adjust to *their* needs rather than the other way round. They might press the claim that their work be made more intrinsically satisfying by being invested with greater discretion. They might increasingly resent their subordination to hierarchical authority and demand increased participation through open-ended forms which go far beyond the manipulative 'human relations' containments currently favoured by some managements.

Claims along this dimension could come to include a demand for effective participation at those highest decision-making levels which determine the aims, conduct and destinies of plants, companies, industries, national economies and the relationships between them. Such aspirations would require for their realisation major shifts in social values and priorities, the structure of power, authority and influence, the distribution of rewards and privileges, and concomitantly no doubt in the patterns of ownership and class stratification. Is it possible to detect stirrings of pressure in any of these directions?

There are few signs of rank-and-file employees aspiring to narrow the ranges of wealth, income and status. The present very great inequalities serve to sustain social values which put predominant emphasis on an acquisitive and competitive getting and spending, and in the absence of any effective alternative vision of how men might live together these will increasingly influence the aspirations and behaviour of the rank and file just as they do those at the top of the hierarchy. It could well be that a severe narrowing of the ranges would both express and reinforce a shift in social values away from competitive acquisition. But leaders of employee collectives do little to offer their members any such alternative vision. Given that present values continue to hold the field and that the enormous permitted variations of wealth, income and status continue to symbolise the value set on competitive acquisition, employee collectives will be expected by most of their members to behave accordingly.

Is there no likelihood of the collectives ever trying to break the vicious circle by seeking to lead members towards the vision of a more equal society? The point here is that no union or even group of unions could hope to pursue such a purpose within the restricted range of one industry or even one sector of the economy. A drive to promote egalitarian values would have to be society-wide. This means, not an industrial movement, but a political movement, using the institutions and methods which that term currently implies, in a campaign for power to effect the necessary institutional changes. Here much depends on the leadership offered by the political movement, for it is likely that many if not most trade unionists see the present range of rewards as an inevitable response to unchangeable laws of human nature, and would need convincing by their political as well as their industrial leaders that an egalitarian programme was viable. Little leadership of this sort has been forthcoming. Equality figures more prominently in political rhetoric than in political programmes. Meanwhile employee collectives, though impelled by values which are nourished and sustained by the existence of very high levels of income and wealth, relate their own aspirations not to these levels but to those more nearly approximating to their own. There seems no present sign of this changing.

About aspirations along other dimensions there is rather more to say. There are some signs, for example, that resistance to the concept of labour as a commodity is stiffening. Following the example of Upper Clyde Shipbuilders there have been less publicised instances where employee groups have occupied factories scheduled for closure. Such groups are aware only of wanting to protect their own jobs and often disclaim any revolutionary or radical political views. Yet the implications of their behaviour are highly political in the sense we examined earlier, for it represents an act of group self-assertion against a principle hitherto considered integral to industrial life in the West – that propertyless wage- and salary-earners must place themselves at the disposal of the changing and fluctuating labour demands of employers and managements – a principle itself highly political, needless to say. Only time can show whether these gestures constitute the early signs of a response destined to grow and strengthen, or whether they are no more than symptoms of a passing mood.

Some commentators profess no such uncertainty with respect to the next dimension with which we have to deal – the degree of active discontent manifested by rank and file towards low-discretion work which affords them little or no intrinsic satisfaction. Confident assertions are made that positive rejection of such work is stiffening throughout the Western world. Reports come in that evidence to this effect is now visible in America and Scandinavian countries, and certainly in France it has been a common talking-point in the 'quality of life' debate since the events of May 1968. It is difficult as yet to gauge the value of these accounts, for many questions remain unanswered. How strong are these responses? Among what groups if any are they prevalent? What priority are members of such groups giving these aspirations as compared with the priority they give to material needs? In Britain the condemnations of fragmented, dehumanised work have hitherto emanated as much from middle-class observers as from the millions of wage- and lower salary-earners who perform it, and as we noted earlier the unions themselves reveal no leadership initiatives designed to awaken or strengthen aspirations in this field of work experience. There are, however, signs of a gathering discussion on the subject, and there is certainly increasing documentation of widespread employee consciousness of a poverty of experience in their work. Yet this consciousness tends to be manifested in the form of responses to inquiries by academics or the media, rather than as a spontaneous assertion accompanied by demands for change.

This passivity of employees and their collectives on the subject is an invaluable resource for those anxious to preserve the *status quo* in work organisation and job design. It enables them to counter criticism with the assertions that most rank-and-file employees shun discretion and responsibility and that would-be reformers are merely trying to impose on others their own values and preferences. The likely truth is, as we have seen, more complex. Men who have never experienced intrinsically satisfying work can hardly be said to have 'chosen' intrinsically unsatisfying work. They have been constrained to submit to it by such factors as family, education and expectations acquired through social conditioning and job experience. Since, in order to preserve their mental health, they are likely to adapt to this situation (or, to use alternative terms, resign or reconcile themselves to it), it is not surprising that they fail to exhibit attitudes more characteristic of those whose family, education and social conditioning have given them very different expectations and aspirations. Passivity may, in other words, symptomise an adaptation to what is seen as inevitable, rather than a voluntary choice from among known and understood alternatives. The fact that employees and their unions in Britain are at present advancing few active claims for intrinsic involvement in work is fully compatible with the possibility that many find their work profoundly unsatisfying but do not see significant change as a realistic aim. Accordingly they adapt their aspirations to what they have learned by experience is within reach.

There is nothing inevitable about their maintaining this passivity towards job design. The growing debate about the quality of life will presumably touch the consciousness of increasing numbers of people, especially the young. This could well encourage many to feel that to spend half – or indeed any – of their waking time in fragmented and meaningless work experience is an unacceptable waste of all too short a life. To be sure, their efforts to eliminate or reduce the waste need not take collective forms. A few might opt out. Others would no doubt seek more interesting work, causing management increasing unease at the rising costs of turnover (and of absenteeism and sickness rates, in all probability). Some would continue to accept fragmented, low-discretion tasks but demand higher financial compensation, possibly pushing management into seeking labour economies and capital-intensive technologies. But there seems no reason in logic why employee collectives should not respond to a quickening interest among members in the quality of their own working lives by leading campaigns against management on this issue.

Of one thing we may be certain. Rank-and-file employees will receive no encouragement from employers and managers, from banking, commercial, financial and advertising interests, or from leading politicians of any party, to pursue greater intrinsic satisfaction in work *at the expense* of economic efficiency, productivity and growth. Where they can be reconciled there will be no problem. But where the first threatens the second, the demand for intrinsic job satisfaction is likely to get short shrift, or come under efforts at manipulation towards more 'responsible' objectives. The influences bearing upon us to pay almost any price for efficiency and growth are already, of course, very great. On all sides we are exhorted to produce more in order to be able to consume more, and to consume more in order to be able to produce more. As yet we offer little resistance. Even those among us who are consuming abundantly show few signs of satiation, and there are considerable numbers still far short of this happy state. The forces arrayed against any demand for intrinsic work satisfaction at the expense of efficiency and growth are therefore potent.

Speculative and tentative though this discussion of future possibilities has inevitably been, it has at least alerted us to the possibility that trade unions and organised work-groups do not have to be supportive of the *status quo*. Certainly the continuance of collective bargaining, if that remains a central purpose, requires that they abstain from attacking those entrenched prerogatives which management currently sees as essential to its functions (just as it requires the same restraints of management). But as we have seen, management's definition of these entrenched rights is not fixed and unchanging. Having changed already, they could presumably change further.

The possibility of increasing resistance obviously introduces a crucial consideration bearing on the unions' chances of success in any programme of 'encroaching control'. Nevertheless the point emerges clearly from this as from earlier discussion that employee collectives participating in managerial decision-making can choose either to accept management's current definition of the boundaries of that participation or to seek to extend them. They can choose either to work within the system or to try to change it. Should they seek to press their encroachment on managerial prerogative beyond the furthest extent which management proves ready to accommodate, their strategy would, by definition, threaten the institution of collective bargaining. While this is a conceivable political programme it seems a highly improbable one in the context of modern Britain.

Even on the assumption that employee collectives continue operating within limits acceptable to management, however, the development of collective bargaining along existing lines could still create a threat for our competitive, acquisitive society and its institutions. To this contingency, and with it the third type of challenge, we turn in the next chapter.

Further Reading

ALLEN, V. L. *Trade Unions and the Government*. London: Longmans, Green and Co., 1960.

CHAMBERLAIN, N. W. *Union Challenge to Management Control*. New York: Harper and Row, 1948.

COATES, K. (ed.) *Can the Workers Run Industry?* London: Sphere Books, 1968.

FLANDERS, A. 'Trade Unions and Politics' in *Management and Unions*. London: Faber and Faber, 1970.

HARRISON, M. *Trade Unions and the Labour Party Since 1945*. London: George Allen and Unwin, 1960.

8. Participation, Bargaining and the Wider Society

INTENDED AND UNINTENDED OUTCOMES
OF PARTICIPATION

The argument to be developed in this concluding chapter requires us to begin by drawing a distinction between a threat to the system that is willed and intended; and a threat that is not willed and intended but develops nevertheless out of men's actions. A simple example will help to clarify the nature of the second. In the early days of the motor-car, the institution of unrestricted private motoring created no great social problems, for only the tiniest of privileged minorities were able to engage in it. With the increasing equality of access to it, however, have come immense problems such as pollution, congestion, road costs, wholesale destruction of amenity, and, of course, death and mutilation on a large scale. It is safe to assume that few of the participants will these consequences. The average motorist wills only his private convenience or pleasure. Yet when large numbers engage in the activity the outcomes include social costs of frightening proportions. It is now surely plain that eventually these costs must reach such levels as to compel governments to impose severe restrictions on private motoring.

The shortcomings of this example as an analogy to collective bargaining will soon become apparent, yet it offers some points that are illuminating. In the early phases of our competitive and acquisitive industrial society the number of individuals and groups with power enough to enable them (as landowners, manufacturers, merchants and financiers) to use it, in one way or another, in a private quest for wealth and status was relatively small. Although their competitive struggles and the methods they used to wage them could sometimes injure large numbers of those they employed, these had insufficient power themselves either to fight back or to get their difficulties elevated to the status of 'social problem'. Later, some of these groups were able to mobilize a little power for themselves by collective organization and use it to defend, and possibly improve, their position. For a long time the proportion of the working population able to engage in this aggressive defence of their modest interests remained small and, even during the later periods of long-term membership growth, has fluctuated considerably. It remains true today that the coverage in Britain reveals great gaps. Large numbers even of male manual wage-earners are still unorganized, and among women wage-earners and white-collar employees of both sexes too the scope for unionisation is considerable. Yet although collective organisation is still so incomplete, the self-protective power pressures through which groups seek, sometimes to improve their financial position, often only to defend what they have, already considerably aggravate the inflationary forces now active for so much of the time throughout the industrial world. Added to the inflationary pressures exerted by manufacturers, merchants, financiers, the higher professions and other groups who seek to protect themselves by using their power to raise prices, margins, interest rates, charges and fees, they create or intensify strains on the country's foreign trading position, economic growth, group relations and other aspects of its social fabric. Here, then, we see considerable stresses being created by the increasingly widespread ability of organised groups to engage in aggressive power struggles, either for advancement or for defence (which under inflationary conditions also requires predatory aggression). In other words, the gradual (still far from complete) universalisation throughout society of the capacity to seek to defend or advance one's economic and status position by means of group self-assertion through power threatens problems which did not exist when this capacity was confined to relatively few. Different countries, with their different histories and institutions, experience these problems differently and some find them more pressing than others. Britain, with her great dependence on foreign trade, is among those for whom they have become politically central, since her ability to maintain a rate of economic growth sufficient to satisfy ever-rising private aspirations and ever-expanding public programmes depends on coping adequately with those problems.

COLLECTIVE BARGAINING AND THE BRITISH PROBLEM

But adequate prescriptions depend on a sound diagnosis. How far have we in Britain achieved one? The various attempts made since the Second World War with respect to wage restraint, later incomes policy, have assumed it to be possible to apply such a policy successfully within the existing framework of competitive, acquisitive, pressure-group society and its present inequalities. The impression has been allowed to develop, at each period of crisis, that there was some sense in which the inflationary problem might be permanently 'solved' within the existing framework, thereby making possible sustained economic growth thereafter. It might seem improbable, did we not know it to be true, that politicians could still talk of each latest recurrent manifestation of the chronic contradictions of the system as if it constituted a discrete problem open to some long-term 'solution' which would then set us once for all on the road of steady economic growth. The solution currently favoured, always some variant on the theme of pay restraint, has usually been presented to us as an exercise in economic 'common sense', as if its success depended largely on our grasping certain simple propositions and their self-evident implications. More recently this has been accompanied by the view that for short periods all or some groups might have to be forcibly restrained. One might have supposed that the repetitive failure of this sequence as a long-term solution would discredit the whole approach and prompt a search for a new diagnosis which offered fresh hope. The fact that this has not happened should prompt us to ask why. Why does *homo sapiens*, so brilliantly resourceful in many fields, manifest in Britain towards this particular problem an approach which combines such negligible success with such blinkered and owlish persistence?

One possible explanation is that those with the greatest power to exercise initiatives along alternative lines fail to do so not because they are stupid but because they shrink from the practical measures that might be implied and from the diagnosis that implies them. We shall suggest here one alternative diagnosis and its implications for a long-term public policy.

INFLATION AND THE MORAL STRUCTURE OF SOCIETY

It could be argued that competitive, acquisitive, pressure-group society is coming within range of its own nemesis so far as its manifestation in Britain is concerned. Contradictions exist, of course, in all societies, but those at work here could become particularly threatening. We see a society geared to the notion of a high-consumption way of life, with men urged by a hundred pervasive influences to get and to spend. It is a society wherein relationships are increasingly shaped by the values of commercialism and contract. In respect of large sectors of activity we could characterise it, as we could characterise many others of its kind, as low-trust society. This is manifest at both the organisational and the societal level. Our brief survey of the long and largely vain struggle by organisational management to secure the social integration of the rank and file by evoking their involvement and identification suggests that the large-scale work organisation does not, in the existing social context, command the moral adhesion of lower-level employees. It fails on two levels. Not only does the employee often lack intrinsic involvement in his own task activities; he also feels little commitment of loyalty, responsibility and concern towards the organisation as a whole. In both respects his attitude is more likely to be one of instrumental attachment. In other words, he sees job and organisation largely as means to an end, and in this case the end is the preservation and advancement of his material standard of life (an advancement he is exhorted to pursue vigorously by many influences outside the organisation).

His attitudes towards that abstract entity, 'society as a whole', are not much different. He has but an infinitesimal stake in its distribution of property, status and power of decision-making. Except in war, when the issues are quite different, there are vital respects in which it does not command his moral adhesion. Currently the most important of these relate to inflation. When he sees the material standards of himself and his family reduced or threatened by events within or beyond his society he seeks, perhaps through a collective, to cover himself by encroaching on the standards of others ('One man's wage increase is another man's price increase'). Governments claiming to speak in the name of society as a whole beseech him to restrain himself. But the moral structure of our society is not strong enough to take this kind of strain. It is a characteristic of low-trust society that its members assume everyone else, especially those richer and more powerful than themselves, to be ensuring their own self-protection. They place little trust in the will or ability of either management or government to ensure justice, so they pursue justice strictly for themselves through the process of group self-assertion, using such power and arguments as they can muster. Little or no positive response is offered to exhortations by government, which only achieves a modicum of temporary success the nearer it approaches the notion of a 'deal' or is able to impose a brief moratorium by authoritarian fiat – both of them typical tactics of low-trust situations.

Here we see, then, competitive pressure-group society increasingly bedevilled by the universalising of the values it encourages and the attitudes it generates. The more men are driven to see their work solely or largely in terms of the financial rewards it offers them – and are deprived by the nature of their work situation of the opportunity to develop any intrinsic involvement – the more they will judge and legitimise management solely by that criterion. Similarly, the more government upholds a social system which, through its institutions of private enterprise, profit-seeking, market relationships and massive inequalities, sanctifies and institutionalises material and status self-seeking through power, the less the participants in such a system can be reached by moral appeals from government to restrain their own hand 'for the common good'. Such appeals are tantamount to a demand that men behave in a high-trust manner within what they perceive as a low-trust situation. As we saw in our study of the organisation, such demands are doomed to failure.

DIVERGENT PRESCRIPTIONS

Diagnoses in this vein are likely to seem disagreeable to those whose interests or values are bound up with the continuance of the system in its present shape, for they seem to suggest that a choice has to be made between two prescriptions equally daunting. One follows the analogy of society and the motor-car. If the increasing universalisation of unrestricted private motoring threatens such severe social costs that it must eventually be brought by law under rigorous government control, could not the same be said of unrestricted sectional collective bargaining? The symmetry may seem attractive and will appeal to many. Yet pursued this far the analogy fails on the crucial issue of method. An attempt to bring collective bargaining under authoritarian government control by legislative fiat, leaving unchanged such features of the system as profit-seeking; hierarchy; extreme subordination and division of labour; gross inequalities of power, wealth, income and status; and pressure-group activities of many other sorts; would understandably meet with bitter resistance. Resistance would be justifiable because any such attempt would be totally without moral basis. It has been urged many times by recognised authorities in the industrial relations field that government policies can succeed only if they secure the more-or-less willing compliance and confidence of the greater part of the trade union movement. No such confidence would be extended to a government which upheld all the institutions and values of the competitive, acquisitive, pressure-group society except those which enabled trade unions and their members to protect themselves within this social context. A policy of this kind could only be applied with the methods of the openly coercive police state. Many other citizens besides trade unionists would think ill of this destruction of liberal-democratic freedoms and would extend their displeasure to those proposing it.

Yet if the prescription derived from the motor-car analogy presents difficulties the alternative must seem for some no less unpleasant. The case would be that the existing structure of society and social values is such as to leave us, in certain respects, with little sense of moral adhesion to it, thereby rendering ethical appeals worthless. And if, in the absence of an adequate sense of social obligation, the attempt is made to enforce the desired patterns of behaviour, this is seen to require a major exercise of coercion. Does this not suggest that the alternative may be to plan, and begin to implement, a long-term programme of major social change which stands some chance of promoting a measure of that moral adhesion so conspicuously lacking? If collective bargaining cannot, within our existing social system, be controlled by externally-applied government force, then the only alternative is to seek changes in the system which strengthen the disposition of bargaining groups to control themselves. This would require that they perceive their society in markedly higher trust and justice terms than they do at present. A society which strove towards equality might be able to engender a deeper sense of responsibility and concern for the cohesion, stability and integrity of our corporate life. Within the context of a search for social justice there might be some hope of negotiating with the unions that social contract of which we have heard much in recent years, for the necessary basis of a moral commitment to the corporate life could then exist on which to seek agreement about rights and obligations. This is hardly the place to discuss what measures would be necessary to strengthen, sufficiently for this purpose, the legitimacy of the system in the eyes of the less favoured. We can only note that, since no marginal tinkering would be adequate, it would be foolish to play down the full implications and difficulties of mobilising support for a frontal assault on gross inequalities of wealth, income and privilege.

DOES INCREASING PARTICIPATION NEED A CONTEXT OF EQUALITY?

But while we can properly abstain from discussing practical policies we cannot evade the need to justify the principles of our argument on this point. What are the grounds for believing that equality – the contracting of the extremes of wealth, income and privilege within narrow limits – would sufficiently mitigate the acquisitive group self-seeking which so disfigures our society with its ever-enlarging encroachment on community and trust? Clearly the present argument stands or falls on this belief. It is surely justified by much observation that while there are always a few social predators who must be put down, most social aggression is a form of defence against feared encroachments by others. When men believe they see others gaining a defensive or offensive advantage through an assertion of power they follow suit. In so doing they provide the same cue for action by others, and thus the downward spiral of distrust is reinforced. All the evidence is that the nearer conditions approach to equality of treatment, the easier most men find it to accept limitations to their material aspirations. Obviously for those at the very top of the social structure the situation we are contemplating represents nothing but loss and they could be expected to react accordingly. But for those at all levels beneath this apex the relevant question is whether the pain of limitation would be offset by (1) the knowledge that no other groups were using power or influence to evade limitation; (2) the demonstration that limitation was part of an overall long-term plan to reduce inequality and privilege – a plan covering education, health, housing, sex discrimination and old age, as well as wealth and income; and (3) the discovery that a social contract negotiated on a (relatively) high-trust basis offered a degree of stability which made possible planned economic growth along with a containment of inflation. Those who reject this formula out of hand are under an onus to show how they see our present grossly unequal, low-trust society as coping with the continuing strains generated by our competitive, acquisitive institutions and values. Relevant here is the point made earlier that our political leaders seem loath to acknowledge that the tendency towards gathering inflation is now a built-in feature of our society as at present constituted. They treat each successive crisis as a discrete problem to be 'solved'. The familiar measures are produced – the 'restraint', the 'pause', the 'freeze', the deterrents to growth, the cuts in public expenditure, and all the other techniques of the stop-go brand of economic management. The structural features of economic and social functioning which generate or aggravate these regular crises are left unchanged. The question must inevitably present itself, however, as to how much longer people can accept the repetition of these expedients, invariably accompanied as they are by the proclamation that, once the present balance of payments problem has been solved, sustained economic growth will follow. Does not each successive crisis strengthen the need to search for a permanent adaptation of our economic and social functioning and structure – an adaptation which helps us collectively to contain inflationary tendencies instead of driving us, in our socially divisive, self-seeking groups, to aggravate them? Must we not try to promote among ourselves a sense of social obligation and responsibility towards our common life which offers greater stability than seems likely in the future if we continue along present paths?

IMPLICATIONS FOR THE MANAGER

The broad answers suggested to these questions now need to be examined for their implications with respect to the managerial problems of promoting cooperative compliance and, if aspirations extend that far, evoking moral involvement. The argument has been advanced here that only a long-term radical programme of social equality stands any chance of generating a sufficiently widespread sense of commitment to our common life. But would this commitment include, for the individual, moral involvement in his job and the organisation? Nothing in the arguments just presented made any specific reference on this point. Yet the manager may see it as crucial. It must be said at once that he would be enormously helped in his search for a stable and agreed pay structure (with all that this means for mutual confidence and industrial peace) if he operated within a changed social situation which strengthened men's trust in the equity and fairness of their society and in the policies recommended by their leaders. But such changes would not necessarily include any significant shift in the moral involvement men bring to their actual task activities and to the organisation itself. They may feel satisfied that their pay is fair without necessarily being fired with commitment in these deeper senses. The manager will therefore want to know whether, alongside efforts to strengthen men's moral adhesion to the society which represents their common life, there exist promising strategies for strengthening their moral involvement in job and company. The preceding chapters of this book have argued that, given existing patterns of division of labour, this goal is highly elusive.

Certainly it may be that men's consciousness of living in a far more equal society would lead them to offer a more willing cooperation. Such might be the consequence if rank and file were to see top management not as an embodiment of power, privilege and status to whose interests and purposes they were forced to be unwillingly subservient, but as simply another functional group whose rewards and status did not set them apart and whose purposes were demonstrably directed towards the common wealth and not sectional privilege. Men might then greet managerial decisions, plans and policies with significantly less suspicion and distrust than they often do now, and few managers will need persuading that this would represent for them an important strengthening of their leadership. But optimism must not be over-indulged. Should we seek to maintain our present patterns of division of labour these are likely to set tight limits to what management can achieve in respect of rank and file involvement. Those in the lower ranks of large-scale complex organisations are likely always to have great difficulty, by virtue of their circumscribed functions, responsibilities and perspectives, in fully sharing the values and purposes of those at the top. Changes in technology and job organisation may help management by making possible marginal increases in work discretion which can sometimes engender corresponding increases of intrinsic involvement. But these changes are currently initiated only when higher authority sees them as contributing to, or at least compatible with, the long-term financial or growth interests of the organisation as it defines them. If social values came to give relatively higher priority to the quality of men's work experience and relatively less to the profits, productivity and growth which provide high material rewards, management would find it easier to provide a humane and fulfilling work situation. But as long as we see our present material aspirations as requiring those patterns of division of labour to which industrial society has become accustomed, management will remain profoundly handicapped in that search for employee involvement which we have traced in this book.

However the manager reacts to some of the arguments presented in this chapter he can hardly ignore the questions to which they try to offer answers. Such questions concern the whole social environment within which he operates; the environment which helps to shape the problems with which he has to deal; the motivations, attitudes and values he brings to them; and the motivations, attitudes and values of those he seeks to coordinate, direct and control. These questions concern, therefore, the social meaning and significance of what he is doing. They cannot help but raise issues bearing upon his own social beliefs and what he sees as the desirable shape of society in the future. More important than whether he accepts the particular ideas suggested here is that he should accept the need to think out his position and its practical implications for his role as citizen as well as manager.

Such a process has to begin with his recognition of being a member of a society along with other human beings who are involved one with another in determining the nature of their mutual relations. He may choose to reject the idea of a society of near-equals. Before he does so too hastily, however, he should take into account all the available evidence bearing upon his preference for an unequal society. How does he assess the quality of social relationships between individuals and groups which this kind of society has produced in the past and continues to produce now? What are his predictions in this respect for the future if the present social framework and values continue unchanged?

There are two different criteria to apply in making these evaluations; one of morality and one of expediency. The manager can ask himself whether or not he finds great social inequalities morally offensive. A common response is that such inequalities are not pleasant in themselves but are necessary for effective organisation, efficiency, growth and the stimulation of talent and ambition – in other words that great inequalities are justified by expediency. A plausible case could be made that this has indeed been true for many situations in our industrial past, when spectacular economic advances were made by powerful individuals who drove large numbers of materially and often psychologically dependent people into highly unequal and autocratic patterns of collaboration. Even the manager who rejects equality as a moral principle must now ask himself, however, whether inequality on the present scale in all its various forms is likely to serve as well in the future in terms of expediency. It has just been argued that great inequalities, besides impeding cooperation and compliance by heightening distrust between management and managed, also foster those competitive pressures, offensive and defensive, which aggravate inflation, make an agreed incomes policy even more elusive than it would otherwise be, lead to checks on economic growth, and threaten to generate mounting strains and instabilities in the future. We have also noted earlier those trends in the economic and technological world which, it is said, increasingly require of all participants a willing compliance, flexibility and ready adaptation to new circumstances. The accelerating pace of change in technology, methods and markets is thought to create a growing need for a readier rank-and-file response to managerial leadership. The manager needs to ask himself whether this response is ever likely to be forthcoming from the lower ranks of an organisation which, like the society that contains it, is highly unequal along all the important dimensions of life and experience. All in all, then, a case can be made, simply in terms of expediency as measured by economic growth, financial and trading stability, and capacity for adaptational resilience, that the structural inequalities which created and still uphold Britain's class divisions constitute an impediment destined to loom even larger in the future. It will long ago have become apparent that such is the conviction of the author of this book, for whom equality has emerged as the condition for a politically adult and responsible Britain cohesive and unified enough to withstand the stresses of a rapidly changing world.

Further Reading

CLEGG, H. A. *The System of Industrial Relations in Great Britain.* Oxford: Basil Blackwell, 1970.

CLEGG, HUGH. *How to Run an Incomes Policy.* London: Heinemann, 1971.

CORINA, J. *The Development of Incomes Policy.* London: Institute of Personnel Management, 1966.

Index

Compiled by J. K. Macqueen